# BILLY THE KID

# HIS REAL NAME WAS ....

## JIM JOHNSON

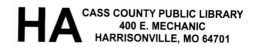
**Outskirts Press, Inc.**
**Denver, Colorado**

Outskirts Press
http://www.outskirtspress.com


ISBN-10: 1-598004-73-5
ISBN-13: 978-1-59800-473-1

Library of Congress Control Number: 2006926557

# DEDICATION

I dedicate this book to my daughter, Heather Nicolle Johnson, who, at the time of the writing of this book, was only 13 years old. She always displayed much needed patience and understanding, and always gave me lots of encouragement. When I would get frustrated, she would lift me up with her beautiful smile and glowing blue eyes, and her positive attitude.

# TABLE OF CONTENTS

# FOREWORD

Who was Billy the Kid? That is a question that no one has ever answered for sure. There have been a lot of speculations and 'facts' that have been printed, but nothing that anyone seems to want to hang their hat on. Most historians and authors seem to think his real name was Henry McCarty and that he was born in New York in 1859. But, this information seems to have come from Pat Garrett's book published in 1882, titled, *The Authentic Life of Billy, the Kid.* The problem with repeating anything from this book is that the book is thought to be mostly fiction. No real proof of this claim has ever been offered, but on the other hand, there have been testimonials from people that lived in New York about the same time that say they remember him as a young, malicious kid. But, are these testimonials really true or was the boy that they remember really someone else.

Most people tend to agree that William Bonney was killed by Pat Garrett on the night of July 14, 1881 at the home of Pete Maxwell at Fort Sumner, New Mexico. But, was William Bonney really killed, and if he was, was he the real Billy the Kid? Was Henry McCarty ever called William Bonney or Billy the Kid? Most historians and authors seem to believe that William Bonney was Billy the Kid., but was he? Some 'proof' does exist that supports that William Bonney was Billy the Kid and that Henry Antrim was William Bonney, but how reliable is this 'proof'. Will the real truth ever be known? We shall see!

# PREFACE

I have been very interested in the Billy the Kid saga since the black and white movies of the 1930's and 1940's. While Billy the Kid was real, the movies were mostly fiction, but they were correct to betray him as a young man who always seemed to be on the wrong side of the law. Was it that simple and clear-cut? How could he get into so much trouble at such a young age? Today, we naturally equate the law as being the side of good and right. What if that was not the case then? It certainly was not the case in and around Lincoln County New Mexico when the Billy the Kid legend unfolded. As you probably know, his situation and the circumstances confronting him were somewhat complicated to say the least.

As I read and researched materials about Billy the Kid, I began to realize that, in most cases, he was nothing more than a product of the circumstances of the place and time in which he found himself. One could even argue that he was a victim of circumstance. In those days, the west was wild and wooly, full of outlaws and ruthless business men working in concert with one another. Laws and their enforcement were often tailored to serve the special interests of men of power and money with little regard to right and wrong. Which side of the law one was on, often depended on where they were and when they were there. Outlaws wanted in one area served as lawmen in another. Lawmen from one locale moonlighted as outlaws in another. Dropped into such a setting, it is not hard to understand how a young boy on his own, might make some bad decisions. Without proper parental guidance, a guardian angel, or a crystal ball, a youngster such as Billy was more or less doomed to fall under the influence of one of the lawless factions. After all, these factions served both sides of the law. The side of the law they served was in the eye of the beholder.

It wasn't always easy to tell the good guys from the bad guys. Right and wrong wasn't always black and white, especially when the rule of law was used by the bad guys to gain an advantage over the good guys. This was precisely the situation in which Billy the Kid found himself in Lincoln

County New Mexico. History would later judge that Billy did fight for the faction that had right on their side. Unfortunately, they didn't have the law on their side. The law was on the side of the corrupt business men.

Both sides employed some pretty unsavory characters. So what's a kid supposed to do? The obvious answer would be to look for work in some place far away from Lincoln County, New Mexico. But Billy didn't have anybody around that would have offered him such advice. He saw two options. He could either support the good guys or he could support the bad guys. He chose the former and I applaud him for it. There would have been no honor in the latter. With the murder of his friend, John Tunstall, Billy knew that he was fighting on the side of the good.

Even though Billy was on the side of right, he was surrounded with associates that spanned the spectrum from very good to very bad. All would have a keen influence on him, and in the end he would be simply a reflection of those with whom he rode, "the good, the bad and the ugly."

Many of the books and articles written about Billy the Kid were filled with fiction and mistruths to try to complement the real truths. Far too many authors depended on nothing more than unsubstantiated lore represented by their predecessors as facts. Troublesome gaps in their stories were often filled with wild embellishments of fact and pure fiction, the spawn of their own overactive imaginations. This, together with the passage of time, has compounded the problem of getting at the real story. Research, for the most part, has become much easier with the coming of the internet and the vast amount of data that is now available. The real challenge, though, is to sort the fact from the fiction, especially when it pertains to Billy the Kid.

Although internet researchers are limited by the information available online, they have the ability to cross-reference that information, communicate with other interested users, and easily locate available records archives that can be researched either online or on site at the location where the records are physically stored. The archives that have to be researched manually on site are voluminous and take hours upon hours to glean meaningful data. In many cases, even scholarly archives contain information extracted from newspapers, magazines, and books that may not be entirely factual.

Other places that can be researched are county and state offices and historical societies. This type of information is usually factual and can be trusted, especially birth certificates, marriage licenses, divorce documents, and death certificates. Historical society archives often contain interviews with the actual players and with people of the era who knew the players.

Interviews with descendants of players or witnesses, two and three generations removed from an event, should be viewed with an abundance of caution. Stories passed from person to person within the same generation invariably suffer an erosion of facts. When passed from generation to generation, such erosion often becomes a mudslide. Whether the interview is that of an eyewitness or that of a descendant, one or more generations removed from the event, one must look to other interviews and documents in order to judge the probable degree of its accuracy. If it passes such scrutiny, then such interviews are invaluable aids that can be used expand known facts.

Did I use information from articles and books written by other authors? Yes, I did. But, the information that I used was either to help substantiate generally accepted facts or to prove that claims represented as factual could be unrealistic and impossible. Some things are easily proven to be true by existing primary source documentation. Absent the luxury of such quality documentation, reasonable theories can be formed when they are the only logical answer to a given set of circumstances.

If something sounds unrealistic, then it probably isn't true. But on the other hand, if it sounds realistic and conforms to a reasonable degree with the known proven facts, then it is possibly true. However, even then, it should be accepted only on its probability and merit. Facts pertaining to events that took place over 120 years ago are very scarce. However, those facts that do exist and that have been proven, serve as a framework within which realistic conclusions can be drawn. In some cases, I have done exactly that, but the conclusions I have reached are not indisputable.

There are many questions to be answered and a lot of supposed preexisting 'facts' that yet need to be proven. In all cases, I have put forth a lot of effort through thorough research in a quest for the truth. I have spent over 40 years reading and researching related publications, thousands of hours on the internet, and thousands of hours of digging through archives. I have interviewed third and fourth generation descendants of the actual people who either participated in or who were present during that period in history. I hope that you read this book with an open mind, relying on your own knowledge, experience, and intelligence to reach your own conclusions as to what is real and what is make believe.

Over the years, since the supposed killing of Billy the Kid by Pat Garrett on July 14, 1881, there have been many old time cowboys that have claimed to be Billy the Kid. Somehow, according to these claimants, Billy was able to escape death, and lived and died in Arizona, California, Nevada, New Mexico, Texas, Old Mexico, or even England. Most of these claims have easily been proven to be false.

The only two claims that seemed to have any substance were those of John Miller and William Henry Roberts. John Miller was born in Oklahoma or Texas and died in Arizona. William Henry Roberts was born in Texas or Arkansas and died in Texas. Roberts used the aliases, Oliver L. Roberts,

Oliver P. Roberts, and Brushy Bill Roberts, but claimed that his real name was William Henry Roberts.

Although John Miller, himself, never publicly claimed to be Billy the Kid, his family and friends 'knew' without any doubt that he was Billy. They gave many believable reasons why they felt that way, but apparently no one ever took the initiative to find out the real truth. John Miller died at the Pioneer Home in Prescott, Arizona on November 7, 1937.

William Henry Roberts was discovered in 1949 by Attorney William V. Morrison. At first, Roberts denied that he was Billy the Kid, but eventually confided in Morrison that he was. William Henry Roberts died on the streets of Hico, Texas of a heart attack on December 27, 1950. He claimed to have been 91 years old when he died.

William Henry Roberts usually went by the name of Ollie L. Roberts or Oliver P. Roberts when he was alive, but has since become better known as Brushy Bill Roberts because of his claim to fame. Brushy Bill amazed everyone with his knowledge of the facts surrounding Billy the Kid and the Lincoln County War, as well as, his resemblance to the Kid.

The first chapter of this book deals with John Miller and what we can piece together of his real life. You will see that John Miller's life was truly fascinating in its own right – Billy the Kid or not. It was fascinating not only for what we do know, but for the mystery that surrounds what we don't know. The stories told by his family and friends were very sincere and are rooted in lore that predates that of other claimants by several decades.

The remaining chapters, with the exception of the last, deal with Brushy Bill Roberts and his claim. His story will be told in its entirety as told to Morrison so that you can judge for yourself, whether his seemingly extensive knowledge of the facts is really accurate. If you have read anything about Billy the Kid or viewed the latest movies in the theatres or the documentaries on television, you will be able to appreciate his knowledge of the events.

Brushy Bill's knowledge of some of Billy the Kid's experiences in New Mexico makes him very believable. The scope and depth of his knowledge as to some of these facts, makes one think that he had to have been there. He made some mistakes, but those could be excused because of his age and the passage of time.

Throughout the chapters on Brushy Bill, I refer to him as Brushy so as not to confuse him with the man he claimed to be. As you know, most people believe that Henry McCarty was Billy the Kid and that he used William Bonney as an alias during the last three years of his life. So, as you read, just remember that I am referring to Brushy Bill Roberts, William Bonney, and Henry McCarty and not necessarily the same person, and not necessarily Billy the Kid. Confusing? Not really as you will see.

Throughout the chapters on Brushy (Chapters 2 through 6), his story, as he told it, is written in normal print. Embedded within these chapters are some generally accepted facts and my comments and conclusions. These are typed in ***bold italics.*** I elaborate on Brushy's stories and then compare his stories to the truth as accepted and documented by most modern day historians and authors, as well as, I present new facts and offer my own conclusions. Please keep in mind the type of print and what is represented by each. This book will be more understandable and meaningful with this in mind.

The story of John Miller was taken primarily from the historical documents available to the general public in archives, census records, death records, and land records. The book, 'Whatever Happened to Billy the Kid', written by Helen L. Airy, was used very sparingly since reliable information could be found elsewhere.

The story of Brushy Bill was taken primarily from the book, 'Alias Billy the Kid', written by C. L. Sonnichsen and William V. Morrison in 1955. The book was used as the main reference guide although many other sources were available. But, I felt these other sources were expanded versions of the original book and contained unverified material, as well as some fabrication. As I mentioned earlier, William V. Morrison was the attorney who actually found and interviewed Brushy Bill. I felt his book contained accurate information taken directly from his interviews with Brushy and from notes that Brushy supposedly had given him. You might want to read his book because it is very convincing and would help you form your own opinion about Brushy's story.

The story told about Henry McCarty and William H. Bonney (Bonny) was taken from many 'reliable' sources, including, but not limited to, books written by some prominent authors and historians. These authors included Frederick Nolan, Bob Boze Bell, William A. Keleher, and Robert Utley. I consider the books written by these authors to be as close to reality as was possible at that time. The 'facts' were not taken from any one book, but derived from areas within all the books where they closely agreed with one and other. Of course, there are still many unknowns and a lot of mystery surrounding the Billy the Kid story. Will they be solved in the future? I hope so. Only time will tell.

Read my book with an open mind. Verify the contents, the facts, evaluate my conclusions, and decide for yourself if either Miller or Brushy was Billy the Kid. Did Billy die in Fort Sumner, New Mexico, or was it in the Pioneer Home in Prescott, Arizona, or on the streets of Hico, Texas, or maybe elsewhere? I have tried to provide you the best available evidence and interpretations of this evidence. You be the judge.

# ACKNOWLEDGEMENTS

There are so many historical societies, county and state offices, and universities to whom I would like to extend my most sincere gratitude. Their names are listed in the bibliography in the back of this book. The Universities that I visited were extremely helpful in directing me to information in their archives. But, as it turned out, very little of that information could be used in the writing of this book.

I must extend a special thanks to the *University of New Mexico Press* for letting me use the information from their book, *Alias Billy the Kid*, written by C. L. Sonnichsen and William V. Morrison in 1955. Their immediate response to my request for copyright permission prevented any delay in my writing this book.

The person that deserves more than just an acknowledgement because of his dedication and desire to find the truth, is my best internet friend, Mr. Charles O. Sanders from Delaware. He played a significant role by using the internet to locate and extract data from genealogy databases and archived historical data. He was able to find information that substantiated some of the most important points in this book.

# CHAPTER 1
## JOHN MILLER
## HIS STORY

John Miller was a Billy the Kid claimant who received very little publicity. He wanted it that way, and for that reason, he is very unique. In fact, it is not entirely accurate and certainly not fair to include him in that group, because he never publicly made such a claim. At times, under the influence of alcohol, he would jokingly say he was Billy the Kid, but then deny it when he sobered up. His friends, family, and associates, who all believed him to be Billy the Kid, only went public with the claim after his death.

So, Billy the Kid or not, we can not blame John Miller for having made the claim - he didn't. Nor, can we thank him for providing any first hand background information that might have accompanied such a public declaration, had he made one. Instead, we must depend on second hand information provided in interviews, his obituary, and a precious few official records.

As you will see, whoever John Miller was, he was one truly fascinating character in his own right. His story has never been thoroughly researched, and his life is therefore more mysterious than Brushy Bill's.

What follows is a summary of pertinent information that has been previously recorded. Is it fact or is it fiction? As you will see, the line between fact and fiction is not always that easy to discern. Where records suggest something different than has been recorded, I have made appropriate comments and observations to that effect. My goal here is not to diminish the works of others, but to further enhance the stories they have told through the introduction of records not relied on by them. Here's what we have – fact or fiction?

It has been stated that on August 8, 1881, less than a month after Billy the Kid was allegedly shot by Pat Garrett, Miller and a woman by the name of Isadora were married in Las Vegas, New Mexico. It's an intriguing story indeed, but did it happen? Maybe, but if it did, it probably didn't happen on August 8, 1881.

In the censuses of 1900 and 1910, John and Isadora were consistent about only one thing, the length of their marriage. In 1900, they stated they had been married 14 years. In 1910, their household was recorded twice. On the first occasion in 1910, they stated they had been married 25 years, and on the second, 24 years. All things considered, it is reasonable to conclude that they were married in 1885 or 1886 and not in 1881. We also learn from the 1910 census that Isadora had been married once before and had two children, one who was still living at that time.

The Millers adopted a Navajo boy sometimes shortly after 1900. The 1900 census shows no children living in the Miller household on June 6, 1900. The two census visits of 1910 both show one adopted son. On one, he is listed as 16 year old Max, a white adopted son. On the other, he is listed as 16 year old Roman, an Indian adopted son. As to the Roman entry, it is more than likely that the census agent erred and should have recorded his name as Ramon.

Was his birth name Ramon or Max or neither? Were both names given to him by John and Isadora? Was Max short for Maxwell? If he was in fact named Ramon Maxwell by the Millers, that would be very intriguing since we find a Navajo Indian with the same name in the 1870 household of Lucien B. Maxwell, father of Pete Maxwell, in whose bedroom Billy the Kid was shot.

In the book *Memories of Cibola*, the author, Abe M. Peña, writes that

**Doa Virginia Perea Sanchez, a midwife, delivered Max Miller, a Navajo who is suspected of having been adopted and raised by Billy the Kid.**

On the 1900 census, there was a Virginia Sanchez living at Penasco, Taos, New Mexico where the Millers lived at that time.

All we know with certainty is that this adopted son of John and Isadora's appears to have gone by the name Max Miller for the rest of his life. He registered for the World War I draft as Max Miller and on that occasion declared he was a Navajo Indian. He is listed in the Navajo Death Records as Max Miller born on January 8, 1894 in Ramah, New Mexico, died September 1, 1988 in New Mexico, and buried in Gallup, New Mexico. He is also found in Social Security records as Max Miller.

In the 1880 census, we find a John Miller living in, Georgetown, Grant County, New Mexico, who, in all likelihood, is our subject. His occupation is listed as a gambler. Some distance away, but still in Georgetown, we also find a 21 year old William McCarty. He was also known to have been a gambler. If these are our subjects, John Miller and Henry McCarty, alias Billy the Kid, there can be little doubt that they knew one another. It would of course also mean that one of them was not Billy the Kid. The odd man out in that case would probably have to be John Miller, but it would explain how John Miller knew so much about Billy the Kid.

John Miller had an old friend named Herman Tecklenburg. It was said that Tecklenburg had known Miller during Miller's outlaw days in Fort Sumner and Oklahoma. This same claim represents Tecklenburg as stating that he had known Miller when Tecklenburg was working as a cowpuncher around Fort Sumner and Miller was the outlaw known as Billy the Kid, who was dodging Part Garrett and his posse. As you will see, these claims will not standup under scrutiny.

Herman Tecklenburg told many people in the area that he knew that Miller was Billy the Kid. His son, John Herman Tecklenburg Jr., remembers Miller visiting his father at their home near McGaffey. John Herman Tecklenburg Jr. said the two old friends sat up most of the night on an outside log, telling stories about the Old Days when his father was a young immigrant from Germany looking for adventure in the old west, and Miller was a young gunslinger fighting the Lincoln County War. There is no reason to doubt that these two old friends did in fact recount the Old Days. However, there is no chance that they had known each other during the Lincoln County War.

The *Gallup Independent* on August 9, 1944, contained an interview of Herman Tecklenburg with columnist Wesley Huff about his life as a frontiersman and his long friendship with Miller:

**They shot somebody over at Fort Sumner and they buried him there and put an end to the hunt for Billy the Kid. But, it wasn't Billy they shot. Billy and his Mexican wife escaped over into Old Mexico, and when I was living at Page about thirty-five years ago, he came with Lou Shoemaker to visit me and we talked over old times. He was ranching down near Ramah. They all knew him down there as Billy the Kid, but never spoke of it for fear of getting him in trouble. He was a prince. The big shots made him out to be an outlaw because they couldn't handle him. Down at Ramah, he was known as John Miller.**

The recollections of Herman Tecklenburg and those of his son, John Herman Tecklenburg Jr., present no problem. They are nothing more than their own recollections of John Miller in and around the turn of the century - which included their sincere belief that John was Billy the Kid. But that belief was not based on Herman having personally known John Miller during the Billy the Kid era. In fact, I am not convinced that Herman ever claimed he did.

Family records show that Herman Tecklenburg was born on June 9, 1869, as Herman John Tecklenburg in Schwarme, Kingdom of Hannover/Schwaner, Hanover Province, Germany. Furthermore, immigration records list him as having immigrated to the United States aboard the SS Nurenburg when he was 14 years old, arriving on June 5, 1884.

Clearly, it would have been impossible for Herman Tecklenburg to have known John Miller as Billy the Kid during the Kid's outlaw days in Fort Sumner and in Lincoln County, which history records as having officially ended on July 14, 1881 in Pete Maxwell's bedroom in Fort Sumner. Tecklenburg was only 13 years old on that date and he lived thousands of miles away. It is certainly possible though that Herman Tecklenburg had met John Miller in the Fort Sumner or Lincoln County area prior to John Miller and Isadora's marriage about 1886.

A neighbor of the Miller's, Eugene Lambson, was interviewed in July, 1976, when he was eighty-eight years of age. When he was asked if he thought Miller was Billy the Kid, he answered positively,

**"I know he was. It was generally understood up around Ramah that John Miller was a fugitive, and most people thought he was Billy the Kid. Herman Tecklenburg, for instance, was a good friend of John Miller and he told us for sure that he knew that John Miller was Billy the Kid. Herman Tecklenburg was an early settler, and owned a ranch up in the Zuni Mountains. Then there was the Crockett family, whose land adjoined the Miller land. All of the Crockett family will tell you that they knew that John Miller was the Kid. In the early years, we probably heard more about John Miller than most people because my sister, Hesseltine Lambson, was dating one John Hill who lived at the Miller place. Hill said John Miller talked a lot about Billy the Kid, but never admitted that he was the Kid. John Hill had a beautiful singing voice, and John Miller could sing pretty well, too, and they liked to harmonize, especially cowboy songs. John Hill never married. Later, he moved to Los Lunas where he ran a service station for many years. John Miller liked to dance, too, and often attended the dances at Ramah where I played the fiddle for community dances, sometimes in the living room of my house. Miller was a good dancer and all the girls were pleased when he showed up at the dances and asked them to dance."**

Eugene Lambson also told an unusual story concerning his father, Appollas Lambson and Pat Garrett.

**"My father was a friend of Pat Garrett when Garrett was stationed at Holbrook, Arizona, and my father was living seven miles south of the town and was selling salt to the Mormon settlers. Pat Garrett told my father about the night he was supposed to have shot the kid at Fort Sumner."**

Lambson's report of the shooting of the Kid by Pat Garrett differed somewhat from the usual accounts of that event. Lambson's version goes like this,

**"Pat Garrett, in the company of his deputies, McKinney and Poe, learned the kid was in Fort Sumner, holed up at the house of Pete Maxwell. They sneaked up to the house in the dead of night, and Garrett knocked on the door. A Mexican youth with a gun in his hand answered the knock and queried, "Quien es?' Sheriff Garrett pushed the door open and fired. The Mexican youth fell dead, and Garrett told the Kid and his girl who was there with him, to pack and leave Lincoln County forever."**

Lambson said that Garrett deliberately allowed the Kid to escape because

**"Garrett and the Kid were friends."**

Garrett didn't want to kill the Kid, and had been dragging his feet about bringing him in. But, because of the killing of two guards when the Kid escaped from the Lincoln jail, the pressure was on the sheriff to do something.

Another neighbor of the Miller's was Atheling Bond who was interviewed in 1978, when he was eighty-nine years of age, at his home on Main Street, not half a block down the street from the Bond Trading Post, which he operated throughout his life, and was then owned by his son, Edgar.

**"John Miller liked to tell stories about Billy the Kid's gun fights, but he did not want us to think he, himself, was the Kid. He would end each story about the Kid's adventures by reminding us that he was not Billy the Kid. However, his wife, Isadora, who could not speak English, would tell us in Spanish that he really was Billy the Kid, and his name was not John Miller. She told us how Billy was shot in Fort Sumner, and how she took care of his wounds, and when the officers came around her house looking for him, she hid him between two straw mattresses which she slid under the bed."**

Shortly before 1920, the Millers moved to Washington, Maricopa County, Arizona, and by 1930, they were living in Liberty, Maricopa County, Arizona. According to Isadora's death certificate, their home burned on October 18, 1936, and she burned to death before she could be rescued.

On March 12, 1937, Miller was admitted into the Pioneer Home in Prescott, Arizona. He had fallen from a roof and his son, Max, felt that he needed to be placed in a retirement home.

On November 7, 1937, John Miller died at the Pioneer Home and was buried in the Pioneer Home Cemetery. His cause of death was listed on his death certificate as a fracture of the neck of the right femur and broncho pneumonia. He was buried on November 9, 1937 in the Pioneer Home Cemetery.

In his interview, Lambson said,

**"One day a stranger from Phoenix, Arizona, walked into the malt shop. He was looking for an heir to John Miller's estate. He told me John Miller had died in Buckeye, Arizona, and since no one there knew of any survivors, the court appointed three men to go through his effects. The man said he was one of the persons so appointed, and when they searched through the contents of an old trunk, they found documents, letters, and other items which convinced them that John Miller was Billy the Kid."**

Lambson said that he directed the man to John Miller's adopted son, Max Miller, but Lambson never learned what happened to the trunk after that. Later, when Max Miller was interviewed about his life as the son of Billy the Kid, he could not remember anything about what happened to the trunk and had no idea where it was.

Another good friend of the Millers, Georgie Conley Jackson, said in an interview that she did not believe that John Miller was Billy the Kid, but stated that he was on the run. She said that she did not remember Miller's wife's name as Isadora because Miller always called her 'Eeh Haw' which was Comanche for 'my love'. Georgie also stated that Miller had told her family that his mother was Comanche and his father was a white buffalo hunter. He also said that he did not have a pair of pants until he was seven years old and that he and his mother lived with the Comanche Indians in Texas until he was grown. He said that the Indians taught him to steal horses and use them.

Georgie also stated that Miller knew Billy the Kid and ran with him on some of his escapades and that he had a horse stealing corral in a canyon in New Mexico. Presumably the ranch in the canyon to which Miller referred

**Cass County Library-
Harrisonville**

**816-884-3483**
2/12/2020 5:08 PM

*Renew your items online at*
*www.casscolibrary.org*

---

## Items Renewed

1. Billy the Kid : his real name
   was--
   Barcode: 0002205752500
   Due: 3/4/2020

---

was the ranch at Portales which Billy the Kid owned in partnership with Charles Bowdre. She said that most of John Miller's doings was horse stealing and he was taught by the Comanche Indians. She said that Miller lived with the Comanche Indians and grew up with them, not New York.

The Sharlot Hall Museum in Prescott Arizona provides online an extract of John Miller's death certificate, to which they have attached a note which reads:

**Adopted as infant by Kiowa tribe after one parent was killed and other burned to death by Indians as a sacrifice. Treated well by Kiowas.**

According to the museum's archivist the note is based on information found in John Miller's obituary in the Prescott Courier. However, the November 8, 1937 obituary to which they refer, reads in part as follows:

**John Miller, who was adopted as an infant or very young boy by an Indian tribe after one of his parents had been killed outright and the other one burned to death as a sacrifice by the Indians, died at 6:30 p. m. Sunday in the Arizona Pioneer Home.**

The obituary goes on to say that John Miller did not know what tribe of Indians it was except that it was not an Arizona tribe. Thus the specific Kiowa and Comanche linkage is still somewhat in question, but it does appear that he lived with one or both at some point in his early life. Whether his mother was Comanche, Kiowa, or white is unknown.

As you can see, separating fact from fiction is not that easy. What is easy is to jump to conclusions thereby creating fiction based on fact. In case there is any lingering doubt as to what is fact and what is fiction concerning John Miller, here is a summary of just the facts as found in official records:

Pioneer Home records in Prescott Arizona state that he was admitted there on March 12, 1937, arrived there on March 14, 1937, and died there on November 7, 1937 at 6:30 PM. They also state that he had come to the home from Maricopa, Arizona; that he had been born in Fort Sill, Texas in December, 1850 (December with a question mark); and that he did not remember his mother's and father's names. The record also contains the rather curious statement that he first arrived in Arizona just after the capture of Geronimo in Phoenix.

John Millers death certificate (see Appendix A) states that he was born in Fort Sill, Texas on Dec 1850 and died at the age of 87 on November 7, 1937 at 6:30 PM at the Arizona State Pioneer Home in Prescott. Cause of death cited as "fracture of the neck of the right femur and broncho pneumonia." His father and mother are listed as unknown.

Isadora's Millers death certificate (recorded under the name Dora Miller, (see Appendix B) states that she was born in Las Vegas New Mexico (no date of birth given) and died at the age of 95 on 18 Oct 1936 at her home in Liberty, Maricopa County, Arizona. The certifying official wrote that he "saw a burned and charred body and believed from widower on hand that said body was that of Dora Miller". He goes on to add "burned to death when her house burned". Her father's name is listed as Sise, her mother's, as unknown.

Census records found as follows:

On June 6, 1900 in Jaralozo, Valencia County, New Mexico, John Miller is listed as born in Texas December, 1857, age 42, married 14 years, and both his parents born in Kentucky. Isadora is listed as Isidora S. Miller, born in New Mexico on December, 1849, age 40 (an obvious error), married 14 years, and both her parents born in New Mexico. Living with them is John Hill, a boarder, age 22, born March 1878 in Ohio (parents also born in Ohio).

On April 15 & 16, 1910 in Jaralosa, Valencia County, New Mexico, John Miller is listed as age 59, married 25 years, and born in Texas as are both his parents. Isadora is listed as Isidora Miller, age 54, married 25 years, and born in New Mexico as are both her parents. With them is Roman (probably should be Ramon) listed as their adopted son, Indian, age 16, born in New Mexico as were both his parents.

The same Miller household was recorded a second time on April 19, 1910, this time recorded as being in Ramah, McKinley County, New Mexico. John Miller is listed as age 58, married 24 years, and born in Texas as are both his parents. Isadora is listed as Isodora Miller, age 58, married 25 years, and born in New Mexico as are both her parents. With them is Max listed as their adopted son, White, age 16, born in New Mexico with both his parents born in Texas. This time Isadora is shown to have been married once before and to have had two children, one still living at that time.

On January 26, 1920 in Washington, Maricopa County, Arizona, John Miller is listed as age 69, born in Oklahoma, with his father born in Kentucky and his mother born in Oklahoma. Isadora is listed as Esadora Miller, age 53, born in New Mexico with both her parents also born in New Mexico.

On April 15, 1930 in Liberty, Maricopa County, Arizona, John Miller is listed as age 80, born in Oklahoma, with both his father and mother born in Missouri. Isadora is listed as Dora Miller, age 84, born in Oklahoma, with both her father and mother born in Missouri.

The following is the full-text of John Miller's obituary as published on page 3 of the *Prescott Courier*, November 8, 1937:

**MAN RAISED BY INDIANS PASSES**

John Miller, who was adopted as an infant or very young boy by an Indian tribe after one of his parents had been killed outright and the other one burned to death as a sacrifice by the Indians, died at 6:30 p. m. Sunday in the Arizona Pioneers' Home.

Because of the circumstances of his childhood he was hazy about exact facts of his life, though he believed he was born in December, 1850 at Fort Sill, which he said was in Texas though there is a Fort Sill in Oklahoma.

Miller did not know his parents' names, the date he entered this state, but believed it was a short time after the capture of Geronimo, or what tribe of Indians it was except that it was not an Arizona tribe. Though the Indians had meted his parents the most cruel death, he remembered them always as being kind to him, though indeed he had to live very long periods of times on nothing more than parched corn and shiver in the winter time in skins. But he did not regard such existence as a hard life unnecessarily because it was all he and the Indians with whom he lived knew.

One time the Indians painted him all up for some sort of ceremonial dance and some of the paint accidentally got into his eyes. It was of a nature that impaired his eyesight thenceforth.

At one time he was married, but whether it was an Indian woman was never determined by those in charge of the pioneers' home. But his married life was short, for once when he was away the house caught fire and his wife was burned to death. He never did explain whether it was accidental.

On October 14, Miller fell at the home and broke his hip. That mishap hastened the end.

He entered the home last March 14 from Phoenix but had lived around Buckeye for a good many years and listed Ralph Watkins, secretary of the chamber of commerce, as a friend. There are no known relatives of course.

The incidents about his life he remembered hazily, and as related here, have been batched together from odds and ends of information told those at the home. He was not a man to make up stories about himself, however, consequently what he has told has been taken as the truth. Burial arrangements are being held in abeyance at the Hunter Mortuary.

These records do provide much information, but they also raise some key questions. They are:

When was John Miller born? His death certificate and obituary both say December, 1850. From 1900 through 1930 he was visited by the census taker five times (twice in 1910). His age as given in four of those five visits (1910 through 1930) reflect his birth year as 1850 to 1852. Only in 1900, is he outside that range when he claimed a birth date of Dec 1857. Thus, it's probably pretty safe to toss out the 1857 date, and conclude he was born about 1851. That is of course if John Miller in fact had any idea of when he was born. That's a big "if" considering the circumstances surrounding his early life.

When was Isadora Sise Miller born? Her birth date is a little tougher than John's. Her death certificate gives no date of birth, but it does state that she died at the age of 95 on October 18, 1936. That computes to a birth year of 1841. The data from the five census visits from 1900 through 1930 reflect a birth year anywhere from 1846 to 1867. The 1867 date is so far out of line that it can easily be tossed. On two of the remaining four censuses, John was successful in claiming he was younger than Isadora, which strongly suggests that he was. Having established Johns birth year with some confidence as about 1851, then Isadora's was in all probability at least two to four years earlier, maybe even earlier. My "guess" is that it was about 1846, give or take a couple of years.

Where was John Miller born? It's fairly obvious that he told the Pioneer Home that he was born in Fort Sill, Texas. Even the author of his obituary was perplexed by this declaration. Fort Sill is a problem in two respects. First, it's in Oklahoma and it's always been in Oklahoma or Indian Territory as it was formerly known. Secondly, Fort Sill was not named as such until July 2, 1869, when Camp Washita (also known as Camp Medicine Bluff) was renamed Fort Sill in honor of Brigadier General Joshua W. Sill. Furthermore, Camp Washita had only recently been established in January of 1869. Before that there was no fort by any name on the site that was to become Fort Sill. And that site was never in Texas.

However, Fort Sill is in present day Comanche County, Oklahoma, and Comanche County is separated by only one county from what was once Greer County, Texas to the west. Greer County, Texas included all the land between the Red River and North Fork of the Red River. Texas, initially laid claim to this territory in 1860 and it remained in dispute until 1896 when the United States Supreme Court ruled against Texas and Greer County became part of Oklahoma. The territory that was Greer County of 1896 includes all of the current Oklahoma counties of Greer, Jackson, and Harmon and that part of Beckham County south of the North Fork River.

It is also interesting to note that all of the disputed territory, that was early Greer County, as well as that to the east which included the site of Fort Sill, was all within the land known as Comancheria. This of course was the land of the Comanche, and it was land shared by the Comanche with their neighbors just east of Fort Sill, the Kiowa.

Thus, we have all the ingredients of the John Miller story in the neighborhood of present day Fort Sill, to include a piece of Oklahoma that was once Texas. So when John Miller said he was born in Fort Sill, Texas, did he mean on the precise site that was to become Fort Sill in 1869 Indian Territory (Oklahoma)? Or did he mean near Fort Sill at an unnamed location in what would become Greer County, Texas in 1860, and finally Greer County, Indian Territory (Oklahoma) in 1896?

It is interesting to note that John claimed Texas as his birth place in 1900 and 1910, but in 1920 and 1930, he changed it to Oklahoma. Did word that the United States Supreme Court had awarded Greer County to Oklahoma reach John 20 or so years late?

Was John Miller really Billy the Kid? I think not, but you make up your own mind. There is a lot of evidence against him, the most telling being his date of birth of about 1850 as discussed earlier. All indications are that Billy the Kid was born between 1859 and 1862. But then John Miller's claim of being born in December, 1857, as found in the 1900 census (unlikely as it is), does make it interesting.

If John Miller was Billy the Kid, then how did he escape from Pat Garrett at Fort Sumner? It is said that Miller told different versions of the escape to his friends. One version is that he was shot in the chest a week or so before July 14 and that Isadora was nursing him back to health when Garrett accidentally killed a Mexican sheep herder in the Maxwell house. Another version is that Miller was shot by Garrett in the Maxwell house and played dead while Garrett inspected him. When he was carried away by his Mexican friends to be prepared for burial, they noticed signs of life and he was hidden and cared for by Isadora. Meanwhile, a Mexican who died a day earlier was placed in the casket and buried. According to this version, Garrett supposedly never learned that Billy was not killed by him.

Keep in mind though that these stories are not first hand accounts related by John Miller, but second and third hand accounts as told by someone who had supposedly heard them from someone who allegedly heard them from John Miller or Isadora. In short, the chain of custody is somewhat questionable.

Did John Miller ride with Billy the Kid? This is very possible if he is in fact the John Miller in the 1880 Georgetown census. If it is, then they would have been in the same places at about the same time and would have known some of the same people. That is assuming of course that William (Henry) McCarty was Billy the Kid.

Was John Miller's real name, 'John Miller'? That is very unlikely since it would appear that not even John Miller knew his real name. It's rather clear he did not know his parents' names.

If you would like to learn more about the actual claims made by John Miller's family and friends, you might want to read the book, *Whatever Happened to Billy the Kid'* by Helen L. Airy. If you read the book, weigh the claims presented therein against the facts presented here. Helen Airy seems to support the John Miller claims in her book, but at times, she also seems to be unconvinced and hesitant to make statements of verifiable facts.

# CHAPTER 2
## BRUSHY'S STORY · IN THE BEGINNING

Brushy's grandfather, Benjamin Roberts, settled in Nacogdoches, Texas in 1835. In 1836, he helped Sam Houston free Texas from Mexico. Brushy's father, J. H. Roberts, was born March 8, 1832, eight miles from Lexington, Kentucky. His mother was Mary Adeline Dunn Roberts who was also born in Kentucky (See Appendix D).

J. H. Roberts and Mary Adeline moved to Texas in the late 1850's and finally settled in the area of the present town of Buffalo Gap. William Henry 'Brushy Bill' Roberts was born December 31, 1859 near Buffalo Gap. Shortly after he was born, his father left to fight in the Civil War. During the Civil War, his father rode with Quantrell's Raiders along with Jesse and Frank James.

J. H. Roberts became known as 'Wild Henry' and 'Two Guns' Roberts. He was a rough and tough cowboy with a very short temper and was known to be as mean as any man alive. He was a former Indian fighter and experienced a lot of violence.

While J. H. Roberts was away fighting in the Civil War, Brushy's mother died in 1862. He was only 3 years old. Some of their neighbors were taking care of him until his dad returned from fighting in the war. While staying with neighbors, Brushy's half aunt, Catherine Ann Bonney McCarty, Mary Adeline's half sister, came from Indian Territory and took him to live with her as her own son. Catherine was a half-sister to Brushy's mother. Catherine changed Brushy's name from William Henry Roberts to William Henry McCarty.

Brushy and his new family left Texas and went to Trinidad, Colorado, then to Santa Fe, New Mexico, and finally to Silver City, New Mexico. His Aunt Catherine covered their tracks well because J. H. Roberts was known to be very abusive to his mother and she did not want J. H. to find them.

When Brushy's father returned home from the Civil War, sometimes after 1863, he found that his wife had died and his son had disappeared. He tried desperately to find Brushy, but to no avail. He remarried in 1864 to a woman by the name of Sarah Elizabeth Ferguson. They had a son, James Roberts, who was born in 1865. He was Brushy's half brother.

*No official records have ever been found to support any of Brushy's claims as to his birthplace or his parents. It is said that a cousin of Brushy's produced a Bible containing handwritten notes supporting some of his claims. Another cousin produced a family tree as support for his story. Where's the Bible and where's the primary source documentation on which this family tree was based? Until these are produced and inspected by an expert, the authenticity of these documents must be considered suspect.*

*Further suspicions are raised by Brushy's claim that his father married first, Mary Adeline Dunn, and then in 1864 he re-married to Sarah Elizabeth Ferguson. It's time to meet Oliver Pleasant Roberts, a supposed first cousin of Brushy's, who was born on August 26, 1879 in Sebastian County, Arkansas. Oliver P.'s father, Henry Oliver Roberts, was also married first to a Dunn (Caroline Dunn). Even more startling is that Oliver P.'s father married secondly, Oliver P.'s mother, a Sarah Elizabeth Ferguson, just as Brushy's father had. This Henry Oliver Roberts family is a matter of public record and is supported by official documents. Of course it would not have been that improbable for Brushy's father, J. H. Roberts, and Brushy's uncle, Henry Oliver, to have both married a Dunn. But it would have been very improbable for both to marry a woman by the name of Sarah Elizabeth Ferguson. Might this suggest that William Henry Roberts, Brushy Bill Roberts, Oliver L. Roberts, and Oliver P. Roberts were probably one and the same person?*

*It's also appropriate here to look at Mrs. Catherine McCarty and William H. Antrim. After all it's Catherine's son, Henry McCarty that Brushy claims to be (only Brushy claims to be her nephew). It is a documented fact that William H. Antrim was living in Indianapolis, Indiana from 1865 until 1870 and there is very strong evidence that Catherine McCarty was living there in 1867 and 1869. There is undeniable proof that they both were in Wichita, Kansas by the middle of 1870 and that they remained there through the end of 1871. There is some evidence that they went to Denver, Colorado, from Wichita. There is no question that they then moved to Santa Fe, New Mexico, where official documents record their marriage on March 1, 1873 with Henry*

*McCarty and Joseph McCarty among the witnesses and listed as "Sons" (See Appendix C). And it is well documented that shortly after their marriage they moved on to Silver City, New Mexico, arriving there in the spring of 1873.*

*Contrast the above facts with Brushy's claim that he and his new family left Texas and went to Trinidad, Colorado and then to Santa Fe and then on to Silver City. Brushy would seem to have forgotten about living in Indianapolis, Indiana and Wichita, Kansas before going to Colorado and New Mexico. How is that possible? Might his age account for these critical omissions? Maybe, but all things considered it seems a bit unlikely.*

In late 1872, Brushy returned to Texas to visit his real family. Upon arriving at Buffalo Gap, Texas, he found that his family had moved to Carlton, Hamilton County, Texas. He left immediately for Carlton. Here, he became known as 'Kid Roberts' because of his small size and youngish looks.

Brushy soon became a good rider, and made cattle drives with his father. He learned to ride, rope, and shoot, while becoming proficient in each. His father raised horses, and Brushy was taught how to break them. His father, Wild Henry, would brag that his kid was going to be a bronco buster. Brushy became so good at it, that there wasn't a horse that existed that he couldn't break.

In early 1874, Brushy picked a four year old black horse for himself out of his dad's herd and broke it. He taught the horse to pace, or single foot, faster than most horses could run. His father sold the horse to a doctor, and in an ensuing argument, his father drew his whip and beat Brushy so hard that it took him a month to recover.

*Brushy said very little about his life up to age 12. He said very little about his dad's family and his mom's family. He said nothing about his personal life. Being adopted by his Aunt and traveling around the wild frontier had to have left some exciting and unforgettable memories. Why didn't he mention them? He must have realized they would have gone far in supporting his claim.*

*As cited above, Henry McCarty is listed as both a witness and son at Catherine McCarty's wedding to William H. Antrim in Santa Fe on March 1, 1873. Brushy never mentioned that he had returned to New Mexico to attend the wedding. Did he just forget this event as well? It has also been mentioned in various interviews that Henry was with the family when they arrived in Silver City shortly after the wedding, in early 1873.*

*Should we give Brushy the benefit of the doubt? Could it be that he hadn't forgotten these events, but that he just failed to mention them?*

Once Brushy had healed, and having experienced his father's ruthlessness, he left his father's home for the last time in May, 1874, at the age of 14. He joined a cattle drive that was headed up through the Indian Territory. He hid in the chuck wagon whenever they approached a town because his father had warned him that he would have the Rangers get him if he ever ran away. Brushy left the wagon train at Briartown, Indian Territory, where he continued northward on foot. He was soon approached by an old man who asked him where he was going. Brushy told him that he was running away from home, where upon, the old man said to him, "Climb up, son. You can stay with me."

*In January, 1874, the first public school was inaugurated in Silver City. Louis Abraham, Harry Whitehill, and Charley Stevens, childhood friends of Henry McCarty's were in attendance and they all confirmed that Henry McCarty was also there. Brushy could have had his dates confused, but that would mean that most of what he said needs to be questioned.*

Brushy now had a place to stay, food to eat, and a job as a sentry for Belle Reed, later known as Belle Starr. He did the chores around the place, when he wasn't watching in the mountains with his field glasses for approaching riders. He also had to take a pack horse and go to town for supplies and ammunition. He made friendly acquaintances with the James boys, the Younger Boys, and many other outlaw people who hid out at Belle Starr's place or who just visited while passing through.

Belle Starr really liked Brushy, and seeing how good he was with a six-shooter or rifle, offered him a job as her right-hand man. When Brushy told her that he didn't like outlaw life, she told him that he could leave anytime he wished. When Brushy decided to leave, Belle Starr gave him some nice clothes and fifty dollars. She took him close to town, saying goodbye to the 'Texas Kid', and telling him that he always had a home with her.

Brushy left the Indian Territory and went back to Silver City where his Aunt Catherine and Joseph lived. On September 16, 1874, his Aunt Catherine died from the tuberculosis. He had gotten back in time to be with his aunt before she died. She had been the only real mother that he had ever known. Brushy was now almost 15 years old.

*Henry McCarty's childhood friends said that Henry sat by*

*Catherine's bedside for the last six months of her life. The same friends said that Henry loved Catherine very much and it really hurt him to see her sick. They said he did everything he could to make her comfortable. If these first hand accounts are accurate, then Brushy could not have been in Oklahoma at this time, at least not if he were Henry McCarty.*

*Remember that according to Brushy, he left his father's place in May, 1874 and joined a cattle drive. He left the cattle drive once they reached Briartown, Indian Territory and worked for Belle Reed for three months. So, sometime in late August or early September, he left Belle Reed's ranch and headed for Silver City. This would have been a few days ride. He said he arrived back in Silver City just in time for Catherine's death.*

*If Brushy is to be believed, then somebody had their dates wrong. Was it Henry's childhood friends or was it Brushy? School records as well as records of Catherine's death prove that Henry's childhood friends were right as to their recollection of the dates. If Brushy had his dates right, then he could not be Henry McCarty since these eyewitnesses placed Henry in school in January, 1874 and at his mother Catherine's side for the last six months of her life. Conversely, Henry's friends could not have known Brushy since he claimed to have stayed in Texas from 1872 through 1874. Did Brushy just have his dates confused again? That would be a little hard to accept since these events were so closely related in time to Catherine's death, the one date about which there can be no confusion.*

*Another undisputable fact is that Belle Reed was living in Scyene, Dallas County, Texas with her parents at the same time that Brushy claimed he was staying at her ranch in Oklahoma. Belle's husband, Jim Reed, was involved in crimes in Texas and Belle did not approve of his way of life. She was not involved in crime at that time, nor was she an outlaw, nor did she have a ranch in Oklahoma. Her husband, Jim, was killed on August 6, 1874, near Paris, Texas by J. Morris of McKinney, Texas. Brushy claims to have still been with Belle at the time her husband was killed, but he makes no mention of the killing. Did he just forget that event as well?*

After the death of his aunt, Brushy returned to the Indian Territory and fell in with a bunch of cattle rustlers. He had to clean and polish their boots, clean up their saddles, and anything else they needed done. They beat him and swore that they would kill him if he didn't do what they wanted. One of the rustlers liked Brushy and gave him a small gun to protect himself. His boss liked him, too, and gave him a horse and a saddle.

One morning, Brushy left the ranch for Dodge City, and at the end of five days, he arrived there. He went straight to the wagon yard to leave his horse and to find something to eat. There were four men sitting by a camp fire eating supper, and they invited Brushy to eat with them. One of the men said, "Son, you have a nice hoss and saddle there." Brushy replied, "Yes, and a high bucker, too."

The next morning when Brushy brought his horse out for a rub down, his horse began to buck at the end of his lariat. One of the men that he had eaten supper with said, "Son, you cannot ride that hoss. There's not one in twenty that can." Brushy said to him, "I rode him here. I'll ride him away." "Well son, if you ride that hoss, you need not look further for a job. You already have one with me." He handed Brushy ten dollars and said, "Son, make yourself to home. We'll be leaving here in about four days. We're starting on a long trip to the Black Hills of South Dakota."

It is hard to follow Brushy's account of the next few months. He fell into the company of a man called Mountain Bill, who decided to make a career of betting on Brushy's skill as a rider. Brushy and Mountain Bill covered practically the whole west. They were in Arizona, Montana, Oregon, Wyoming, and Nebraska. No horse was too much for the 'Texas Kid', and he attributed his success to the fact that Mountain Bill had placed him with a band of Cheyenne and Arapaho Indians for training.

Around the April 1, 1877, Brushy and Mountain Bill went to Arizona to visit Bill's sister. They worked a few months on the Gila Ranch. Brushy left Mountain Bill at the ranch and went down to Mesilla, New Mexico, where he ran into Jesse Evans and the boys that he had known before. He had met Jesse in Silver City about 1870 or 1871 and went with him down into Old Mexico after he left Silver City.

*Henry McCarty never met Jesse Evans in Silver City about 1870 or 1871 because he did not get to Silver City until the spring of 1873 and he certainly did not go with Jesse down to Old Mexico after he left Silver City. Brushy may have, but Henry McCarty sure didn't.*

*After Catherine's death, William H. Antrim left for Arizona Territory and left Henry and his younger brother, Joseph, with the Knight family and then later, with the Truesdell family.*

*In late April, 1875, Henry became friends with George Schaefer, an older local boy, who went by the nickname, Sombrero Jack. Sombrero Jack was known to be a mean and ruthless kid.*

*On September 23, 1875, Henry McCarty was jailed in Silver City, New Mexico for stealing clothes from a Chinese laundry. It has been said that he did not steal the clothes and that he was just hiding them for Sombrero Jack. A couple of days later, Henry escaped through the chimney of the jail. Sheriff Whitehill said afterwards that he just wanted to scare Henry.*

*Henry is said to have gone directly to Clara Truesdell's house. She gave him some of Chauncey's clothes and sent him up to Ed Moulton's sawmill on Bear Mountain near Georgetown. Sheriff Whitehill found out where Henry was staying, but before he could get there, Henry left and returned to the Truesdell home.*

*The next morning, Mrs. Truesdell gave Henry all the money she had and put him on a stage to Globe, Arizona. It has been said that he looked up William H. Antrim who was working in Arizona at the time, and when Henry told William what had happened, William told him to leave.*

*Brushy never mentioned his escapades in Silver City and Georgetown. He said he left for Indian Territory after his Aunt Catherine passed away.*

*Most historians agree that Henry being put in jail in Silver City started him on his outlaw career. Why was it not important enough for Brushy to tell about?*

*After Catherine's death, historical records clearly place Henry McCarty in Arizona where he worked as a cook, stole horses and saddles from the Army, rustled cattle and tried his hand at gambling. There is no record of him going to Indian Territory.*

*On March 19, 1876, at the recently decommissioned Camp Goodwin near the San Carlos Apache Reservation, Henry helped himself to a horse belonging to a Private Charles Smith and headed out for Fort Grant.*

*On April 21, 1876, Henry went to work for Miles L. Wood as a cook and waiter at Wood's Hotel de Luna, located just outside of Fort Grant, Arizona. Wood, besides owning the hotel, was also the local Justice of the Peace.*

*Henry teamed up with a man named John R. Mackie and together, on February 12, 1877, they stole three horses at Cottonwood Springs, Arizona.*

*On February 17, 1877, Henry was arrested at Globe, Arizona and taken to Cedar Springs. Somehow, he managed to escape.*

*On March 25, 1877, Henry and John Mackie arrived at the Hotel de Luna for breakfast. The hotel owner and local Justice of the Peace, Miles L. Wood, saw them enter and decided to capture them. He did capture them and walked them two and a half miles to the Fort Grant guardhouse. That night, while a dance was being held at the fort, Henry was left unguarded for a few moments, and escaped.*

*In the summer of 1877, Henry worked for H. F. 'Sorghum' Smith at his hay camp.*

*On August 17, 1877, Henry got into a scuffle with a blacksmith by the name of Frank P. 'Windy' Cahill outside of the dining room of the Hotel de Luna near Fort Grant, Arizona. During the scuffle, Henry was able to get his pistol out and shoot Cahill.*

*The proprietor of the hotel and the Justice of the Peace, Miles L. Wood, witnessed the shooting. He conducted the inquest whereas the coroner's jury declared the killing "as criminal and unjustifiable". He immediately arrested Henry and placed him in the Camp Grant post guardhouse. Henry escaped a few days later, mounted a horse belonging to John Murphey, and headed for New Mexico. A few days later the horse was returned to Murphey.*

*When Henry left Arizona, he went to the ranch house of the Knight's who were friends of his. Their ranch was about 40 miles south of Silver City. He was made welcome by the Knight's; however, the ranch was used as a stage station and was constantly visited by travelers between Silver City and the mining camp at Ralston. Perhaps realizing that it was only a matter of time before his presence at the ranch would become known and that his sanctuary there would embarrass his hosts, Henry left after two or three weeks. Mrs. Knight gave him a horse and he rode off toward Mesilla Valley.*

*While in Arizona, Henry had became known as Kid Antrim, yet Brushy never mentioned it. In fact Bushy never mentioned any of the events that took place in Arizona. One would think that his killing of Cahill and his use of the alias Kid Antrim would be worthy of some mention. Brushy also never mentioned that he had been arrested a couple of times in Arizona and that he escaped each time.*

*Brushy seems to have had a real problem with dates and places. But, we must remember that he was old and it had been over 70 years since these events had taken place. Of course, he did say that he was in Arizona, as well as, Montana, Oregon, Wyoming, and Nebraska between September, 1874 and April, 1877. But, Henry McCarty never left Arizona until after he had killed Cahill.*

Brushy met Mel Segura right after he met Jesse Evans. Jesse and Brushy had stayed at the ranch of Segura's uncle in Chihuahua State, Old Mexico. When Brushy broke Segura from jail at San Elizario, they rode to Segura's uncle's ranch in Chihuahua, where they hid for a few days. Segura went down into Old Mexico and Brushy rode back to Mesilla. That was the summer of 1877. He met Jimmy McDaniel, Billy Morton, Frank Baker, and Tom O'Keefe there.

In the summer of 1877, Tom O'Keefe and Brushy left Mesilla for Loving's Bend near Phoenix, New Mexico. They had a run-in with Indians in the Guadalupe Mountains and Brushy got lost. He lost his horse in the mountains during the fight. He ended up at the Jones Ranch at Seven Rivers. His feet were all cut up from walking days through mountain brush.

*Brushy, again, seems to have forgotten (or more likely was unaware) that Henry McCarty didn't leave Arizona until late August, 1877 and could not have been in Mesilla in the summer of 1877.*

Jim and John Jones were working for John S. Chisum, so Brushy went to work for him. Frank McNab was the foreman, and Tom Storey, Miles Fisher, Walker, Goss, Black, and Ketchum worked there. They made a cattle drive to Dodge City that fall. This was the time that they had a group tintype picture made in Dodge City.

Brushy left Chisum and went to work for Maxwell for a short time at Bosque Redondo. Then, he went to work for Frank Coe on the Ruidoso River. While there, he ran into Jesse Evans and Baker again. They took Brushy to Murphy's cow camp in the Seven Rivers. Evans and his gang stole cattle and horses from Chisum. They still had some of the horses when Brushy went to work with them at Murphy's Seven Rivers camp that winter.

Later on, Brushy and Evans got into an argument about Brushy's share of the bunch of cattle they had cut out and one of the horses that Brushy was supposed to get. They backed out of the deal. Baker accused Brushy of stealing the little roan that he had bought from Chisum. Brushy pulled both his six-shooters on Baker, but Jesse knocked the right one down. Brushy swung the other gun over with his left hand and held it right into Jesse's ribs. Jesse told his boys to keep still or suffer the consequences and begged Brushy to leave peacefully.

Jesse and Brushy had been good friends and nearly like brothers. They had roamed New Mexico, Arizona, Texas, and Old Mexico together. Jesse and Brushy argued, and Brushy almost killed him one day in Lincoln, but he always felt close to Jesse. Brushy had tried to spring Jesse from jail in Fort Stockton one time after he killed a man named Chapman. Henry almost killed Baker and Morton that time.

When Brushy left Murphy's Seven Rivers camp, he rode toward Tunstall's ranch on the Feliz. He was on his way to Coe's place and stopped at Tunstall's to get something to eat. Dick Brewer was foreman, and Bowdre, John Middleton, Doc Scurlock, Bob Widenmann, and many others were there. Brushy told Dick Brewer, a friend of Coe's, that he was headed for Coe's place because he had had trouble with Murphy's men. Tunstall told Brushy that he might as well stay there, so he hired him to ride for him. That is how Tunstall and Brushy's friendship started.

*During his short stay at the village of Mesilla, it may be, as some say, that Henry McCarty met the notorious John Kinney and some of the Jesse Evans' contingent. However, it is more likely that it was later in Lincoln County New Mexico that he joined in their activities. There is no evidence to support the story that in Silver City, Henry, then a schoolboy, had been a 'chum' of Jesse Evans, a man six years his senior. Nor is there any evidence that the two were ever associated with each other at any other time.*

*At Mesilla, one bit of evidence seems to bear out the belief that Henry was still going by his stepfather's name. Eugene Van Patten, a Mesilla valley rancher, was reported as being greatly surprised to learn later that the boy named Antrim, who had come to his ranch seeking work in the early fall of 1877, turned out to be the notorious William Bonney.*

*Henry reached the Jones ranch at Seven Rivers around the 1st of October, 1877. Therefore, he could not have been with Jesse Evans in Grant County on October 9, 1877 as some say. It is certain that he was not with the Evans gang after they crossed the Rio Grande and rode on to the Pecos valley; Henry, by practical accounts, started toward the Pecos with one companion, a stranger named Tom O'Keefe, whom he had met at Mesilla. And he was certainly alone when he reached the Jones ranch house at Seven Rivers.*

*George Coe mentioned that Henry had come to his ranch and spent most of the winter of 1877 with him. If this was true, Henry would not have had time to make a cattle drive to Dodge City, work for Chisum, Maxwell, Frank Coe, and Murphy, as well as, George Coe, before going to work for Tunstall. No date has ever been established as to when Henry reached Tunstall's Ranch, but it would have had to have been in time for he and Tunstall to become good friends before Tunstall was murdered, February 18, 1878. Some witnesses in interviews said that he got to Tunstall's sometimes in January.*

*Some people say that Henry, for reasons unknown, only started using the alias 'William Bonney' after arriving in Lincoln County, New Mexico. As of yet, there has been no viable explanation for this name change or why he picked the name Bonney. Brushy never mentioned that he ever went by the name of William Bonney. How could he have not thought this little detail worthy of mention? After all, he was arrested, tried, convicted, shot, and allegedly buried as William Bonney. He even signed at least ten letters as William Bonney.*

*Brushy said that he tried to spring Jesse Evans from jail in Fort Stockton after he had killed a man named Chapman. There are two problems with this claim; Jesse never shot Chapman and Bonney never got word that Jesse was in jail in Fort Stockton. Later on, Brushy says that he told Governor Wallace that he and Tom had seen Campbell and Dolan shoot Chapman in cold-blooded murder. Brushy just can't keep his stories straight.*

Tunstall had a store in Lincoln in opposition to Murphy and Dolan. McSween and John Chisum became partners with Tunstall. Murphy's men had been rounding up John Chisum's cattle and selling them to the Army at Fort Stanton. Then Chisum would pay Brushy and his friends a dollar a head to get his cattle back. That is how the cattle war got started. Tunstall was pulled into it through the McSween and Murphy troubles. McSween had worked for Murphy as his lawyer, so when McSween joined forces with Chisum, the trouble got worse.

The Murphy group had arrived in Lincoln before McSween and Tunstall got there. Murphy and Dolan had been filling government contracts for beef and provisions. McSween was hired by Murphy to prosecute the Chisum cowboys for cattle rustling. McSween found out that Chisum was only taking his own cattle from the Murphy boys, so he quit Murphy and started up with Tunstall. Tunstall had come from England to settle in this country. He raised full blooded horses and raised cattle on the Feliz. From this time on, there were two factions fighting to get the business.

The Murphy faction had the backing of the Santa Fe Ring which included Tom Catron, U. S. District Attorney, and his brother-in-law. Sheriff Brady was a Catron man. He had threatened to kill Tunstall several times.

Tunstall and McSween were ranching together on the Feliz ranch of Tunstall's. McSween was taking care of the estate of a man named Fritz. He collected on an insurance policy, and Murphy claimed that Fritz was a former partner of his at Fort Stanton and owed money to him. Murphy had gotten a judgment against McSween and started picking up partnership property of Tunstall's. Tunstall turned his cattle over to the law. He had a herd of horses and he decided that it would be best to surrender them to the law until the case was over.

# CHAPTER 3
## BRUSHY'S STORY
## THE LINCOLN COUNTY WAR

On February 18$^{th}$, 1878, Tunstall asked Dick Brewer, Widenmann, John Middleton, and Brushy to accompany him on the drive of the horses to Lincoln. While they were on their way to town, a sheriff's posse, headed by Billy Morton caught up with them in the mountains. Tunstall's men tried to get him to make a run for it as they were outnumbered. Tunstall said that he didn't want to leave the herd of horses and that the posse wouldn't harm him anyway. They killed Tunstall in cold blood and then rode on to Lincoln. None of Murphy's men were present at the funeral when he was buried behind the Tunstall store. Brushy swore that day that all of the guilty men would be killed.

*There are many versions of the death of John Tunstall, but most historians agree to the following version. At dawn on February 18$^{th}$, 1878, Tunstall and six other men; Dick Brewer, Bonney, John Middleton, Rob Widenmann, Henry Brown, and Fred Waite left with the horses. After about ten miles of riding, Waite split from the rest of the party and headed for La Junta. The rest of the group took a short cut through Pajarito Springs. Somewhere along the way, Henry Brown's horse threw a shoe and he had to return to the ranch.*

*Around five o'clock in the afternoon, and only about ten miles from Brewer's ranch, Tunstall, Bonney, Brewer, Widenmann, and Middleton, rode down a gorge that led to the Rio Ruidoso. In front of the pack of horses were Tunstall, Brewer, and Widenmann, with Bonney and Middleton to the rear. Bonney and Middleton suddenly heard the sound of horses behind them. They turned and saw a posse approaching. The duo raced forward, shouting to Tunstall, Widenmann, and Brewer to run for it. At the same time, the posse opened fire on all five men. Widenmann and Brewer followed Bonney and Middleton as they ran for cover in a ravine. However, Tunstall froze, even though Middleton had yelled directly at him to run. The four men lost site of Tunstall.*

*The posse ceased fire and Tunstall rode toward them hoping to talk. As he approached, Billy Morton shot him through the upper chest, the bullet severing an artery and exiting through the center of the right shoulder blade. Mortally wounded, Tunstall fell face down on the ground, at which point Tom Hill shot him in back of the head, the bullet entering behind the right ear and exiting above the left eye.*

*On February 22nd, 1878, at 3 P. M, Tunstall's body was laid to rest in a grave beside his store. The pallbearers were Dick Brewer, Frank Coe, George Coe, and John Newcomb. Bonney and Fred Waite were unable to attend since they were still in jail after being arrested by Sheriff Brady. As Tunstall's body was lowered into the grave, Dick Brewer vowed that he would catch every man that was involved in Tunstall's murder.*

*The murder of Tunstall is generally conceded to have been one of the most unforgettable and damaging events in Bonney's life, yet Brushy gave only a short description of what happened. Brushy should have known how important it would be for him to elaborate on the sequence of events that day if he were to present a convincing story, but he didn't. At least, you would have thought that the interviewer, Mr. Morrison, would have interrogated Brushy more on this pivotal life changing event. Bonney and Tunstall were good friends and it is even said that Bonney looked up to him as a father figure. That alone should have given Brushy the incentive to discuss the death of Tunstall in detail.*

Judge Wilson swore in Dick Brewer as constable and gave him a warrant for the arrest of the murderers of Tunstall. Dick selected Brushy, Henry Brown, Fred Waite, Charlie Bowdre, Frank McNab, and a few others to help him. The hunt began for the murderers who had left Lincoln for their hideout in the Seven Rivers region. As Brewer and his men approached them, the fight began. Some of them got away, but Billy Morton, the leader of the mob, and Baker were captured. They spent the night at Chisum's ranch.

*Historical records show that on March 1st, 1878, Justice of the Peace Wilson appointed Dick Brewer as deputy constable and handed him the warrants for all of Tunstall's killers. The rest of the posse was made up* of Bonney, John Middleton, Doc Scurlock, Fred Waite, 'Big Jim' French, Henry Brown, Charlie Bowdre, Jose Chavez y Chavez, 'Dirty Steve' Stephens, John Scroggins, 'Tiger Sam' Smith and others. John Chisum 'loaned' his cattle detective, Frank McNab, to the posse. The posse members called themselves, 'The Regulators'.

Late in the afternoon on March 6th, 1878, the Regulators spotted Buck Morton, Frank Baker, Dick Lloyd, Tom Cochran, and one other unidentified man in a cluster of trees on the Rio Penasco just below Bob Gilbert's ranch. When the five men spotted the Regulators, they mounted their horses and took off toward Beckwith's ranch. As the Regulators gave chase, the five men broke into two groups, with one made up of Morton, Baker and Lloyd. All thirteen Regulators elected to pursue this group and began firing their pistols at them as they ran.

After running for about five miles, Lloyd's horse collapsed underneath him. However, the Regulators overlooked him and continued to pursue Morton and Baker, allowing Lloyd to escape on foot. After about another mile of running, the horses of Morton and Baker also gave out, forcing the two men to take cover in a cluster of tule reeds bordering the Pecos. After Brewer's threat to burn them out left them no other option, they both decided to surrender. The two men were put on their tired horses and the Regulators began leading them north to Lincoln.

The Regulators, along with their prisoners, continued to follow the Rio Pecos north and stopped at the ranch of Bob Gilbert. At the Gilbert ranch, there was a man by the name of William McCloskey, a former Tunstall ranch hand and close personal friend of many of the men who were in the group that murdered Tunstall, including Morton and Baker. Later in the day, as the Regulators left the Gilbert ranch, McCloskey joined them, saying he wanted to go to Lincoln as well. The Regulators disliked McCloskey and did not trust him, but they allowed him to accompany them on their way to Lincoln.

Late in the Day on March 8th, 1878, the Regulators arrived at the Chisum South Spring ranch. The Regulators and their prisoners were then fed dinner and elected to spend the night. John Chisum's niece, Sallie Chisum, gave up her bedroom for the prisoners to sleep in since it had no windows for escape.

At some period during their stay, the Regulators heard a rumor that Jimmy Dolan was putting together a massive party that would ambush them and free Morton and Baker on their way to Lincoln.

Again, Brushy provides very little information on these events. It could be because of the elapsed time since the events took place, but I think he feels that he is less likely to make a mistake if he keeps it brief.

*Regardless of the reason, he leaves out a lot of pertinent information. One important fact that I would have thought Brushy would have mentioned is that they called themselves 'The Regulators'.*

The next morning, they arrived at Roswell and decided to take the north road over the mountains because they knew that Murphy's men would be waiting for them on the main road to Lincoln. They stopped at Agua Negra, in the Capitan Mountains, where an argument started between one of the posse and Frank McNab. McNab killed the man during the argument. Morton and Baker tried to make a run for it, so Brushy killed them both.

*The next morning the Regulators left and headed for Roswell. They arrived at Roswell around 10 o'clock where Morton was allowed to mail a letter to his family. The Regulators left Roswell and headed west towards Lincoln. A few miles from Lincoln, the Regulators, remembering the rumor about Dolan's party ambushing them, left the main trail and began traveling on an unused trail that took them through Agua Negra Canyon. A short time later, while still in the canyon, Morton, Baker, and McCloskey were killed. There are many different versions of how the killings occurred, but the most probable is that McCloskey tried to assist Morton and Baker in making an escape and all three were gunned down.*

*For some unknown reason, Brushy never mentioned McCloskey by name or who murdered him. He did say that McNab got into an argument with one of the posse and killed him, but never mentioned his name. Brushy seems to be speaking as a man trying to recall a story he's heard or read, rather than telling a story he participated in first hand.*

Sheriff Brady was looking for Brushy to serve warrants for cattle stealing. He caught up with the posse at Seven Rivers and arrested Brushy. He took Brushy's six-shooter, a .44 single action with pearl handles. Brushy had just paid twenty-five dollars for them in San Antonio. Brushy got out on bond, but Sheriff Brady said that he didn't have the pearl-handled six-shooter. He gave Brushy one with wooden handles.

Brushy knew that Sheriff Brady had other warrants and would be looking for him again. In the afternoon of April 1st, Sheriff Brady, his deputy, Hindman, and County Clerk, Billy Mathews, were coming down the street from Murphy's store to the old courthouse. Henry Brown, John Middleton, Fred Waite, and Brushy were behind an adobe wall alongside Tunstall's store.

*This event actually took place in the morning around 9:30 AM and not in the early afternoon as Brushy stated. Brushy should have remembered that it was a cold morning with sleet falling rather than early afternoon.*

*Brady left the House with four deputies, George Peppin, Jack Long, George Hindman, and Billy Mathews, and headed east down the street. Brushy never mentioned Peppin and Long. And, actually there were six Regulators behind the adobe wall, Bonney, Fred Waite, John Middleton, Henry Brown, Frank McNab, and 'Big Jim' French. Brushy also seems to have forgotten that Jim French and Frank McNab were members of his gang that day.*

Mathews and Brushy had a run-in the day before, but Brushy's bullet missed him. As they passed the along wall, Brushy leveled down on Mathews, but again, he missed him. The other men with Brushy were firing at the same time, and Sheriff Brady fell dead on the spot. Hindman died soon afterward, but Mathews got away and ran behind an adobe wall down the street. Fred and Brushy jumped over the adobe wall that they were behind and ran into the street where Sheriff Brady was lying. Brushy pulled his pearl-handled .44 off his body in time to catch a bullet from Mathew's rifle from behind the adobe. Brushy and Fred Waite got back over the adobe wall and headed out of Lincoln.

*I am not sure where Brushy came up with the story that Sheriff Brady had taken a pearl-handled .44 from him. It has always been said that Brady had taken a Winchester rifle from Bonney. He also seems to have forgotten that it was he and French that went out to Brady's body to retrieve his 'pearl-handled .44' and not he and Waite, and that French had been shot as well as he. Also, French was wounded bad enough that he had to remain in Lincoln to get medical attention. Brushy never mentioned that fact either.*

Three days after Sheriff Brady was killed, on April 4th, came the fight at Blazer's Mill. Buckshot Roberts, a crank, but courageous old man, gave Brushy and his gang more trouble than they could handle. Buckshot was out to get their scalps for the money on their heads. He never fought in the cattle war. He was an outlaw before he came to that area of the country. Dick Brewer had warrants for Buckshot's arrest, but Buckshot killed Brewer. Buckshot was finally killed.

Buckshot was run out of Texas by the Texas Rangers. He ended up in Lincoln County. He had gone over to San Patricio, where Brushy had a house, with Murphy's gang to run them out. Then a few days before he came to Blazer's Mill, he stopped at Brushy's house in San Patricio and started an argument with Bowdre. Brushy ran him off, but he came back later as Charlie and Brushy were leaving. He shot at Brushy and Charlie, but he missed.

*Roberts shot 4 or 5 Regulators including Middleton, hitting him in a lung, George Coe, taking off his trigger finger, Scurlock, and Bonney. Brushy doesn't find any of these wounds worthy of mentioning, not even his own.*

*Various sources have said that Andrew L. 'Buckshot' Roberts' real name was William (Bill) Williams and that he had ridden with the Texas Rangers and was later run out of Texas by the Texas Rangers. Who was this Bill Williams? Did he live in Brown County, Texas? The following is extracted from an article from 'The Handbook of Texas':*

On a December morning in 1873, Bill Williams and his son left their home on Sand Creek to cut rails along Jim Ned Creek; after Williams left, his wife took her infant to their cow lot to do milking. While building a fire to keep the baby warm, Mrs. Williams was attacked by the Kiowa renegade Big Foot and his band. The band dragged the baby through the fire, plundered the Williams house, and kidnapped a twelve-year-old daughter hiding inside. Riddled with arrows, Mrs. Williams regained consciousness, took her baby to the house, and treated it's burns. The Williams boy returned to the house on an errand to find his mother dead and the baby dying. After a quickly formed posse trailed the band northwestward, they discovered the twelve-year-old hanging from a cottonwood tree. This and other such incidents prompted the formation of Company E of the Frontier Battalion of the Texas Rangers. The company's commander, Capt. William Jeff Maltby, recruited Mr. Williams and during the following summer camped several weeks along the banks of Sand Creek, from where he and his company patrolled neighboring counties. Eventually, Maltby, Williams and others trailed Big Foot and destroyed him and his band.

*The following was extracted from another article from "The Handbook of Texas":*

After the beginning of the Mason County War and the killing of Moses Baird in September 1875, Ringo and a man identified as Bill Williams rode to Jim Cheyney's home and killed him in revenge for luring Beard to his death.

*It is very possible that 'Buckshot' Roberts was the same Bill Williams mentioned in the previous articles. Ringo was arrested on December 27, 1875 in Burnet, Texas. Williams disappeared at that time and it is possible that he headed for New Mexico to avoid any further confrontation with the Rangers and, once there, assumed the alias of Andrew L. Roberts.*

The three-day battle in Lincoln, July 17, 18, and 19, 1878, was the end of the struggle for the McSween faction. John Copeland was appointed sheriff to succeed Brady. He served until he was removed by the governor. Dad Peppin, who worked for Coghlan, was appointed to replace him. Brushy and his men would drive horses up to Tascosa, Texas to sell, and then they would drive cattle back for Coghlan to buy.

Jimmy Dolan ran the Murphy store in Lincoln in the Murphy building. They had large cattle interests and were selling to the Army and the Indian agency. They would steal the cattle from Chisum and then Brushy and his men would get them back.

Brushy was friends with Chisum until Chisum lied to him over that cattle business. Chisum promised to pay Brushy and his men, a dollar a head to get his cattle back from Murphy. Chisum did not pay off. Also, in the cattle war, he and McSween promised to give them $500 apiece to fight for them.

McSween had been hiding out at the Chisum ranch. Murphy's men had threatened to kill him. Brushy and his men went to Chisum's ranch to bring McSween back to Lincoln. The sheriff's posse followed them and a big fight broke out. Brushy and his friends won the battle and took McSween back to Lincoln.

As they rode into Lincoln, Peppin and his posse attacked them again. The real battle broke out when Brushy and his friends took over Montana's house across the street from the tower where Peppin's posse was holed up. Some of Brushy's friends went into Tunstall's store and the rest went into McSween's house next door. Peppin had filled Murphy's building with his men and he put men on the hillside just south of town.

*The battle in Lincoln has normally been referred to as the Five Day Battle since it lasted five days from July 15th through July 19th, 1878. Brushy called it the Three Day Battle as though he had been misinformed and left out two important days of the battle.*

*Also, Brushy stated that he and his men were fired on by Peppin's men as they rode into Lincoln. Actually Bonney and his men rode in after nightfall and were not detected by Peppin and his men.*

*Brushy stated that he and some of his friends took over Montana's house while others went into Tunstall's store and the rest went into McSween's house next door. Most historians believe that the Regulators actually split up more like the following: About six Regulators took over the McSween house. Also, in the McSween house were McSween himself, Susan McSween, Elizabeth Shield and her children, and Harvey Morris, a young law student who had come to New Mexico hoping the climate would relieve his tuberculosis. Taking over the Tunstall store directly next door to the McSween house were three regulators. Also, in the Tunstall store were Dr. and Mrs. Ealy and their two children, and school teacher Susan Gates. On the opposite side of the street in the Montano store were Bonney and seven or eight other Regulators and about twenty-five Hispanics.*

*In the house of Juan Patron were a few more Hispanics. In the Ellis house, the building on the farthest east end of Lincoln, were about nine Regulators. The horses were located in the corral located directly behind the Ellis house.*

*When the posses of Kinney, Powell, and Turner rode into town from the west after being out searching for the Regulators, they left their horses in the Wortley Hotel corral, and fired several shots at the McSween house. Hearing the shots, Bonney and five or six Regulators from the Montano house ran across the street to the McSween house, while firing their guns at the Dolan men. It is believed at this time, that Bonney, Jim French, Joe Smith, George Bowers, Jose Chavez y Chavez, Florencio Chaves, Vicente Romero, Ignacio Gonzales, Francisco Zamora, Jose Maria Sanchez, Yginio Salazar, and Bonney's new and inseparable sidekick, Tom O'Folliard were in the McSween house.*

On the last day of the battle, Colonel Dudley rode into town with his black soldiers. He demanded that McSween stop the fighting. Brushy and his friends told the Colonel that Peppin and his men started the fight, so go and stop them, and that they were going to protect themselves as long as the posse was going to shoot at them. The Colonel told McSween that he couldn't interfere, and that the sheriff had the matter in his hands.

*The first thing Dudley did was ride to the Wortley Hotel, where he met Peppin and informed him that he and his men were only in town to protect noncombatants, women, and children. He goes on to tell Peppin that he would treat both Dolan's men and the Regulators exactly the same and if either side fired in his men's direction, he would annihilate them.*

*Dudley and his men then continued to ride east through Lincoln and passed by the McSween house, yet Dudley did not stop to tell McSween the same thing he told Peppin. Brushy said that he talked to the Colonel, but Bonney never talked to him because the Colonel did not stop at the McSween house.*

Peppin and his posse set fire to the McSween house to smoke them out.

The fighting continued all day anyway. While the house was burning, Mrs. McSween entered Dudley's camp and begged him to stop the fighting. He told her that he did not have the authority to interfere. But, earlier that day, some of his soldiers were on the side of the hill firing at them.

*The widely accepted story goes like this: Seeing how the Dolan men were getting ready to burn down her house, Sue McSween decided to ask Dudley in person for military protection for her home. She crawled on her hands and knees and once she was at a safe distance from her home, she stood up and walked toward Dudley's camp. Upon reaching the camp, she introduced herself to Dudley, who tipped his hat to her. When she asked him why he and his men were in town, he replied that they were there only to protect the women and children. She then asked why he wouldn't protect her, her sister, and her sister's children, all of whom are still in her house. Dudley replied that he wouldn't protect anyone who willingly remained in the same house with such men as Bonney and Jim French. Mrs. McSween returned to the house and told her husband and the Regulators what Dudley had said.*

By dark, the house had burned except for the kitchen, which was nearly gone. About dusk in the evening, a little after dark, Brushy and his friends decided to make a run for it. The women had already left the house. The building started caving in around them.

There was a window in the east side of the kitchen. The door opened on the northeast corner into an area between the house and the adobe wall. There was a board fence between the house and the corral, running north and south, with a gate at the northeast corner of the yard. Tunstall's store building was east of the board fence on the other side of the corral where we kept the horses. Some of Murphy's men were just across the river, which ran past the north of the house. The gate in the board fence opened to Tunstall's store.

When Brushy and his friends opened the back door to look out, Bob Beckwith and some of the black soldiers started to come in. Harvey Morris, who was studying law with McSween, stepped out of the kitchen door first. Brushy was right behind him and Jose Chavez was behind Brushy, followed by McSween, Romero, and Samora. Morris was shot down in front of Brushy. Brushy ran through the gate with both .44's blazing, and Jose Chavez was right behind him. Jose and Brushy ran toward Tunstall's store, and they were fired at, so they then turned toward the river. A bullet went through Brushy's hat as he went through the gate, and he lost his hat and one of his six-shooter's as he crossed the river. There was brush and undergrowth along the river that gave him some cover.

They had all left the house together, but McSween, Samora, and Romero were driven back by bullets when they reached the gate. They turned and ran back to a small enclosure between the house and the adobe wall, where Bob Beckwith was standing as Brushy ran out the back door earlier. Brushy shot at Beckwith and may have killed him with one of his bullets. They started for the gate the second time, but were driven back to the small enclosure where all three were killed by John Jones, John Kinney, and Dudley's black soldiers. O'Folliard, Salazar, and the rest of Brushy's friends started through. All of them escaped except Salazar, who was cut down by the door. They thought he was dead. He crawled out that night after the posse had left.

*The following is the version accepted by most historians and authors: At the request of Susan Gates, she and the Ealys were escorted from the Tunstall store by three of Dudley's soldiers to a safer location west of town. At the same time, with only the east wing of the McSween house still standing, the Regulators and McSween decided it would be best if Sue and the Shield family left the house. As the soldiers escorted the Ealys past the front of her house, Sue ran out and begged Captain Blair to escort her and her sister's family to a safe location. He agreed and escorted them to the Patron house, which was no longer in the danger of fire.*

*Throughout the rest of the day, hundreds of gunshots were fired. By nightfall, McSween suffered a complete mental breakdown. He simply sat with his head in his hands and muttered to himself. At this point, Bonney assumed command of the Regulators.*

*By around 9 o'clock, only one room of the McSween house remained; the Shield kitchen, located at the eastern end of the building. It was clear that the men inside had to make a break from the house. Bonney quickly devised a plan of escape; he and four others would run through the eastern gate towards the Tunstall store to draw the enemies' fire. This would create a diversion and allow McSween and the others to run north, through the back gate, and to the bank of the Rio Bonito, where they would be safe.*

*Bonney, Big Jim French, Tom O'Folliard, Jose Chavez y Chavez, and Harvey Morris all ran out of the house on Bonney's signal. They made it only a few feet, however, when they were spotted and fired on by the Dolan men. Just as Morris reached the eastern gate, a bullet hit him in the head, killing him instantly. Bonney, O'Folliard, French, and Chavez jumped over Morris' body and continued to run, while firing at their enemies. At the same time, McSween's group made a break from the house and headed north towards the back gate.*

*As for the McSween's group, they were fired on almost the second they left the house. They scattered in all directions, except McSween who froze in one spot. He called out that he wanted to surrender. Deputy Beckwith, one of the men in the backyard of the house, called out to accept McSween's surrender and started to approach him. As he did, someone cried out that he would never surrender, and suddenly Beckwith took a bullet in the right wrist and right eye, killing him instantly. The other Dolan men in the yard, John Jones, Marion Turner, Joe Nash, Andy Boyle, and the Dummy, responded by opening fire on McSween, shooting him five times in the torso.*

*Meanwhile, Francisco Zamora and Vincente Romero ran for McSween's Chicken house, but both men were gunned down once inside, with Zamora being shot eight times and Romero three. Young Yginio Salazar then took a bullet in the back and in the shoulder, that made him fall to the ground unconscious. Ignacio Gonzales was hit in the right arm but kept running.*

*George Bowers, Joe Smith, Jose Maria Sanchez, and Florencio Chaves were the only ones left and they managed to make it through the Dolan men in McSween's backyard and to Bonito's bank, where they found safety. With that, the gunfire came to a halt. The McSween faction had been beaten, and the Dolan men celebrated throughout the night.*

*Hours later, after all the Dolan men were gone, Yginio Salazar crawled to his sister-in-law's house, located a half a mile outside of town. There, he received medical attention. With McSween now dead and the Regulators thoroughly defeated, the Lincoln County War was over.*

# CHAPTER 4
## BRUSHY'S STORY
## THE LINCOLN COUNTY WAR AFTERMATH

Brushy met Tom O'Folliard at Gallegos's house in San Patricio a few days later. They stayed at Brushy's house in San Patricio for a while and tried to work on a ranch. He and Tom wanted to settle down, but it was too late for that. They were now outlaws, so they had to live like outlaws.

Brushy gathered up some of the boys and hung around Fort Sumner, picking up cattle which belonged to anyone who could round them up. They were accused of stealing cattle. Murphy and Chisum were stealing them, too. The only difference was that they were stealing them at wholesale and Brushy and his friends only took them as they needed them. They figured that they had a right to live, so they made sure they did.

With Tunstall and McSween dead, Chisum thought he could get out of paying Brushy and his friends. They told him that if he didn't pay them that they were going to run off enough of his cattle to pay what they thought he owed them. They cut the cattle out of his herd and he did nothing about it.

Brushy tried to get Chisum to pay them, but he told Chisum the quickest way that he could do it was too slow. Brushy had his six-shooter in his ribs, but didn't pull the trigger. From then on, Chisum was his most bitter enemy.

The country was full of bad men in those days. The only difference between them and Brushy was that they had the law and politicians on their side. The law was as crooked as the rest of them.

Brushy was accused of killing a clerk, Joe Bernstein, at the Mescalero Agency on August 5, 1878. Brushy denied killing the clerk. He also was accused of stealing horses from the reservation. He denied that, also.

*The generally accepted story goes this way: Around August 5, the remaining nineteen or twenty Regulators rode to the Mescalero-Apache Reservation Agency, probably with the intent to steal better horses. They split into two groups, one made up of the Anglos, and the other, the Hispanics. Unexpectedly, the Hispanic group was met with resistance by a group of Apaches, and a gunfight ensued. When Agency Clerk, Morris Bernstein, rushed into the battle, he was shot and killed by Regulator Atanacio Martinez.*

*Meanwhile, the group of Anglo Regulators, including Bonney, managed to get to one of the corrals unnoticed. They threw open the gate, and made off with all the horses. By this time, the Hispanic group had left the scene of the gunfight and both groups of Regulators soon met at Frank Coe's ranch.*

*Brushy denied stealing any horses, and never admitted being there. Bonney was there and he helped steal the horses.*

The President removed the governor from office in Santa Fe and appointed General Lew Wallace to the position. Mrs. McSween and Chisum talked to the governor about the conditions in the country. It looked like things were going to straighten out. The governor issued a Proclamation of Amnesty to most of the people involved in the cattle war, but it didn't apply to Brushy. There were indictments against Brushy for the murder of Brady and Hindman.

*It is hard to believe that Brushy actually forgot for which murders he had been indicted. He said that he had been indicted for the murders of Brady and Hindman. In reality, Bonney was indicted for the murders of Brady and Buckshot Roberts.*

Most of the fall and winter, Brushy and some of his friends stayed around Fort Sumner and Portales. In the winter of 1879, they met with Dolan and Evans and agreed to quit fighting each other. When Brushy and his friends were leaving the saloon that night in Lincoln, they ran into Chapman, the lawyer for Mrs. McSween. Campbell and Dolan killed him in cold blood.

*The generally accepted version of the story goes like this: Shortly after dark, February 18, 1879, the first anniversary of the murder of John Tunstall, Bonney, Tom O'Folliard, Doc Scurlock, George Bowers, and Jose Salazar hid behind an adobe wall on one side of Lincoln's only street. On the other side of the street, behind their own adobe wall, hid*

*Jimmy Dolan, Jesse Evans, Billy Campbell, Billy Mathews, and Edgar*
*Walz (Tom Catron's brother-in-law).*

*No one on either side was going to step into the open, for fear they*
*would be shot. Finally, Jessie Evans yelled out that his party should kill*
*Billy on site, to which Bonney responded, "I would prefer not to open*
*negotiations with a fight, but if you come at me three at a time, I'll whip*
*the whole bunch of you!" Walz then bravely stepped out into the middle*
*of the street and managed to calm both parties down and convinced them*
*all to come out in the open. All the men shook hands and decided to go to*
*one of the town's saloons to formally discuss the terms of the truce.*

*In the saloon, a written treaty was made, with six conditions. First, no*
*one from either party may kill someone from the other party without first*
*giving notice of his withdrawal from the treaty. Second, anyone who has*
*acted as an ally of either side is not to be harmed. Third, no harm is to*
*come to any military personnel who aided either side in the war. Fourth,*
*no member of either side is to testify against someone from the other side.*
*Fifth, if any member from either side is arrested, other members from*
*both sides must do all they can do to aid in his resistance, or his release if*
*he is jailed. Sixth, if anyone partaking in the treaty fails to live up to it's*
*conditions, he must be killed.*

*With the treaty completed, all participants decided to celebrate and*
*ordered several drinks in the saloon. With most of the members now*
*drunk, they headed over to the house of Juan Patron who had recently*
*returned from a trip to Las Vegas.*

*Shortly thereafter, the party left Patron's house and headed to Frank*
*McCullum's Oyster House and Saloon, which had been recently built*
*adjacent to the McSween house ruins. On their way to McCullum's, the*
*party ran into Huston Chapman in the street. Campbell stopped*
*Chapman and began antagonizing him, until at one point, Campbell*
*pulled his pistol and stuck it into the lawyer's chest, ordering him to*
*dance. Chapman refused to dance. At that same moment, Dolan's rifle*
*went off either hitting the ground or Chapman, and Campbell shot*
*Chapman in the chest killing him instantly.*

*Brushy said that they were leaving the saloon when they ran into*
*Chapman, but they had actually left the saloon earlier and gone to*
*Patron's house. It wasn't until they left Patron's house, that they ran into*
*Chapman. This is only a slight variation, but it adds further doubt to*
*Brushy's story.*

Brushy got word that Governor Wallace had offered a thousand dollars
to him if he would come in and testify. Brushy wrote him back and told
him that he would come in if the governor would annul those indictments

against him. The governor wrote back that he would meet Brushy at Squire Wilson's house in Lincoln.

Brushy tied his horse up while Tom watched and went up to the back door. The governor and Wilson were alone in the house. Brushy went in and talked for several hours. Brushy told the governor that he and Tom had seen Campbell and Dolan shoot Chapman in cold-blooded murder. The governor wanted Brushy and Tom to testify before the grand jury. Also, he wanted Brushy to testify against Colonel Dudley in his court-martial trial at Fort Stanton. Brushy told the governor about things in general in that area of the country and what started the trouble. He was not afraid to talk like the rest of them and he had the guts to help the governor.

The governor promised to pardon Brushy if he would stand trial on his indictments in district court in Lincoln, testify before the grand jury in the Chapman case, and testify against Colonel Dudley. Brushy promised to do it and, he and Tom left for San Patricio, where Tom lived with Brushy.

Governor Lew Wallace sent Sheriff Kimbrel to San Patricio to pick up Brushy and Tom. The Governor had let Brushy pick the men that he wanted to arrest him. Tom and Brushy went with the Sheriff back to Lincoln and were placed in jail.

*On March 12, 1879, Governor Wallace received a letter from Bonney telling Wallace that he would testify against the killers of Mr. Chapman if the Governor would annul the indictments against him. On March 15, Governor Wallace responded to Bonney's letter, telling him to meet at Squire Wilson's home the following Monday at 9 PM.*

*On March 17, Bonney met the Governor at Squire Wilson's and they agreed that Bonney would testify at the trial and in return the governor would let him go free with a pardon in his pocket. Bonney also agreed to remain locked up for the duration of the trial so as not to arouse suspicion. On March 21, the Governor sent Sheriff Kimbrell and a posse to pick up Bonney and Tom O'Folliard. The two were arrested about a mile south of San Patricio.*

When Brushy's case was called, Judge Leonard was not there. The Court appointed Colonel Fountain to represent him. Brushy pled not guilty to the indictments.

Brushy and Tom went before the grand jury that brought in the indictments against Dolan and his men. Brushy also testified at Colonel Dudley trial in Fort Stanton. Then, they wanted to take Brushy to Mesilla for trial on his indictments.

Brushy had promised the governor that he would only stand trial in

Lincoln and nowhere else and the governor had agreed. It appeared to look now like the governor could not do like he wanted. The judge was a Murphy sympathizer and a friend of Tom Catron at the head of the Santa Fe Ring. Brushy saw that they were not going to treat him right. He went to Kimbrel and told him to give him his scabbards and six-shooters. Kimbrel told him that he could not blame him as it looked like he was being taken for a ride. Brushy did ride, but not to Mesilla. Instead he and Tom walked out of the jail and rode to Fort Sumner.

*On June 17, 1879, Bonney had become fed up waiting for Governor Wallace to come through with the pardon he had been promised, so he and Tom O'Folliard walked past their guards and out of the Patron house. The men saddled up and rode out of town, heading north towards the familiar area around Fort Sumner.*

*Brushy said he went to Sheriff Kimbrel and told him to give him his scabbards and six-shooters, as if he was in charge of the situation. I am sure that it wasn't quite that direct. "Scabbards and six-shooters' sounds like the old western movies.*

*Mr. Morrison stated above, "When Brushy's case was called, Judge Leonard was not there. The Court appointed Colonel Fountain to represent him. Brushy pled not guilty to the indictments." I am not sure what Mr. Morrison is referring to with this statement. A. J. Fountain was not involved in the case against Bonney until Bonney's trial in La Mesilla the spring of 1881.*

There was a good deal of skirmishing after Brushy and Tom walked out of the jail at Lincoln. As Brushy increased the tempo of his activities as a cattle and horse thief, the law speeded up its efforts to catch him. He and his friends were at Greathouse's ranch when they were surrounded by a posse. They sent Carlyle in to get them to surrender. Carlyle had no warrant, so they wouldn't surrender. The posse had Greathouse with them. When the posse commenced shooting, Carlyle got scared and jumped through a window. As he went through the window, the posse shot him without warning. They thought it was Brushy trying to escape and they opened fire. The posse left and Brushy and his friends got out that night.

The next morning, the posse returned and burned the house down thinking that Henry and his friends were still inside. They were going to burn them out just like they did at the McSween house. But, they were beaten again.

Brushy and his gang went to Las Vegas where Brushy read that he had killed Carlyle. He wrote Governor Wallace and told him that he did not kill

Carlyle and that his own men had killed him.

Pat Garrett had been a deputy under Sheriff Kimbrel. Kimbrel ran for re-election. John Chisum, Lea, and several others put Garrett against Kimbrel. They knew that Kimbrel was a friend of Governor Wallace and a friend of Brushy. Garrett won the election.

Pat Garrett had not been in the area long. He came from Texas where he killed a man, a partner, in a quarrel over dividing buffalo hides. Garrett had nothing when he landed in Fort Sumner. Brushy and his friends bought him the first pair of boots he owned in this country. They also paid for the celebration at his first wedding in Fort Sumner. Garrett had rode with Brushy and his gang, gambled and danced, but now he had turned coat.

Garrett went to work for Maxwell when he landed in Fort Sumner, but he didn't last long. He bought in with Beaver Smith, who had a saloon and lunch room in Fort Sumner. The people around there had no use for him, but they were all our friends.

*On October 6, 1880, Bonney wrote a letter to Ira Leonard stating that he wanted to stop running from the law and would like to obtain the pardon promised to him by Governor Wallace. Leonard showed the letter to Wild, who was in White Oaks, and proposed that they use Bonney as a witness against some counterfeiters, and in return finally grant Bonney his pardon. Wild agreed to this and Leonard hastily wrote a note to Bonney telling him to come to White Oaks within the week so they could meet.*

*Some six weeks later, on November 20, 1880, Bonney arrived in White Oaks and went to Ira Leonard's house. However, he found out that he was too late as the lawyer had left White Oaks a few days earlier and was now in Lincoln.*

*Why Brushy never mentioned this opportunity to get the pardon that he had been promised by Governor Wallace is kind of strange. A token pardon seemed very much on his mind in 1950, so why wouldn't he have mentioned this real pardon offer?*

*On November 2, 1880, Pat Garrett, who was in Roswell, was elected Sheriff of Lincoln County, beating incumbent Kimbrell by 141 votes. However, Pat could not take office until January 1, 1881, so Kimbrel appointed him as deputy and took a back seat to allow Garrett to basically act as sheriff.*

*On November 23, Bonney and Billy Wilson met up with Dave Rudabaugh and they headed towards the relative safety of the Greathouse-Kuch station, forty miles north of White Oaks. Before dawn on November 27, a thirteen man posse from White Oaks, led by Will*

*Hudgens and Tom Longworth, surrounded the Greathouse-Kuch way station, which was currently housing Bonney, Rudabaugh, and Wilson.*

*Jim Carlyle was a member of the posse. He was sent inside to try to get the gang to surrender. For some reason, the posse started shooting and Carlyle panicked. He jump through one of the front windows and was gunned down by the posse. Bonney was blamed for the shooting.*

*Brushy did not elaborate on his activities between June 17, 1879 and October 6, 1880. Oddly enough, not much is known about what Bonney did during that same period either. Official records don't tell us; neither do the witnesses to that era. Is it merely coincidence that Brushy also omits this period? Or could it be that Brushy just didn't know what happened during this period simply because very little about Bonney's activities during this same period was ever published?*

With the killing of Carlyle tacked on him, Garrett had another excuse to go after Brushy, which he did. Brushy and his gang were riding to Fort Sumner one night in a snow storm that December about eight o'clock. Garrett and his posse took over Bowdre's home and were waiting for them to come in. O'Folliard had been living with Bowdre and his wife. As Brushy and his gang rode in, Brushy took a different road, thinking they may be watching them. Tom and the rest of the gang rode up to Bowdre's and they started shooting at them, hitting Tom. Brushy heard the shooting and rode in to find the gang retreating.

Garrett and his men carried Tom inside and let him die while begging for water to drink. His cousin, Kip McKinney, one of Garrett's men, wouldn't give Tom a drink.

*On December 19, 1880, Garrett and his men hid in the Indian hospital at Fort Sumner and played cards as they awaited the arrival of Bonney and his gang. Lon Chambers and Lee Hall remained outside on the porch as lookouts. Around 11 P. M., Hall and Chambers spotted six riders coming through the fog and ran back inside to tell the others. The men stepped outside and hid in the shadows around the building, while Garrett and Chambers remained on the porch.*

*Due to the darkness, fog, and the falling snow, the Rustlers could not see the posse waiting for them. As O'Folliard and Pickett rode near the porch, Garrett ordered them to stop. Surprised, the Rustlers instinctively reached for their pistols. Both Garrett and Chambers fired one shot, one of which tore into O'Folliard's chest, knocking him back in his saddle while his horse took off running. The other Rustlers quickly turned their horses around and galloped off as fast as they could, with one bullet hitting Rudabaugh's horse.*

*O'Folliard, who had managed to get his horse under control, reappeared through the fog. The posse approached him and ordered him to throw up his hands, to which he replied that he was mortally wounded and couldn't put his hands up. The posse took him off his horse and carried him inside the hospital building. He was placed on a blanket and the posse resumed playing cards. A few minutes later, O'Folliard died with only one posse member noticing.*

*Meanwhile, a few miles outside of Fort Sumner, Rudabaugh's wounded horse died, forcing him to ride double with Wilson. Pickett went his own way when his horse took off and the other four men continued riding reaching the Wilcox-Brazil ranch shortly after midnight. Believing O'Folliard and Pickett to be dead, the Rustlers considered what their next move would be. Near dawn, Pickett arrived at the ranch and was reunited with the gang.*

After a couple of day's riding in the snow, Brushy and his gang landed at the old rock house at Stinking Springs. They took a couple of their horses inside and tied the others outside from the gable of the roof.

*Most historians agree with the following events: In the early morning on December 20, the Rustlers arrived back at the Wilcox-Brazil ranch. They spent the day in the hills around the ranch waiting to see if Garrett and his men showed up. That evening, the Rustlers went back to the ranch. On December 22, the Rustlers had a meal that evening and decided to leave at once. At some point during the night, they arrived at an abandoned rock house at an area known as Stinking Springs (See Appendix R), about four miles east of the Wilcox-Brazil ranch. The five tired Rustlers made camp in the small house. Bonney took his horse inside with them, while the other three horses were tied to the viga poles jutting from the roof outside.*

*Brushy stated that after a couple of day's riding in the snow, they landed at Stinking Springs. It wasn't a two day ride from Fort Sumner to Stinking Springs. It certainly didn't take Garrett and his posse two days to make the same trip. Garrett and his posse rode out of Sumner after midnight on November 22 and arrived in Stinking Springs before dawn. We know that it took Bonney three days because he spent the better part of the three days at the Wilcox-Brazil ranch. And, it had only taken Bonney a few hours to travel from Fort Sumner to the Wilcox-Brazil ranch which was only four miles from Stinking Springs.*

*Why did it take Brushy two days? And why did Brushy say two days when three days had elapsed between Fort Sumner and his arrival at Stinking Springs? Did he forget he had stopped at the ranch or did he forget having read that Bonney had stopped at the ranch? Or did he just enjoy riding around in the snow; so much so that three days seemed like only two?*

*The Garrett posse rode out of Fort Sumner shortly after the midnight of December 22 and arrived at the house at Stinking Springs before dawn on the December 23. Their trip only took them about 4 hours and this included a detour to Lake Ranch which was about a mile or so off the road and they were also traveling in snow.*

*Brushy also stated that they took a couple of their horses inside and tied the others outside. It is generally accepted that only Bonney took his horse inside leaving the other three outside. Brushy would seem to be wrong as to the number of horses taken inside, and suspiciously vague as to the number left outside. You might ask - who's counting horses? Bonney and his gang were certainly counting horses. They were one horse short. Brushy would have been counting as well and would have remembered the count, had he only been there. Also, for some unknown reason, Brushy never referred to his gang as the Rustlers.*

The next morning at sunup, Charlie Bowdre went out to feed the horses. When he stepped through the door opening, Garrett and his posse fired from ambush without warning, wounding Bowdre seriously. He wore a large hat like Brushy, so they probably thought it was Brushy.

Charlie walked back in, but when he went back after them, he fell dead. The rest of the gang stayed in there all day, planning to ride out after dark. As they were trying to lead the other horses inside, the posse shot one of the horses and it fell over the doorway. The dead horse in the doorway kept them from getting the other horses out.

Garrett promised to protect them if they would surrender. Brushy and his men threw out their six-shooters and filed out the door. The posse loaded them on a wagon with Bowdre's body and took them to Fort Sumner. The next day, they buried Bowdre near O'Folliard, who they had killed a few days earlier.

*According to reliable historical sources, after the Rustlers surrendered, they were given a meal and then loaded onto Wilcox's wagon and taken the Wilcox-Brazil ranch where they decided to spend the night. Garrett sent Brazil, Mason, and Charlie Rudulph back to Stinking Springs to retrieve Bowdre's body. They spent the night at the ranch and around noon on December 24, the posse rode to Fort Sumner, accompanied by Manuel Brazil driving the wagon containing the four prisoners and the body of Bowdre.*

The next day Mrs. Maxwell sent her Indian servant over to ask Pat Garrett if he would let Brushy visit with them before taking him to Santa Fe to jail. Dave Rudabaugh was chained to Brushy, when Jim East, a friend of Brushy's from Tascosa, Texas, and another member of the posse took them over to Maxwell's house. The Indian servant was wearing a scarf that she had just made from Angora goat hair. Brushy traded his tintype picture in his shirt pocket to her for the scarf. He wore the scarf around his head on the trip to Las Vegas after they left Maxwell's house.

After Brushy and Rudabaugh were taken into the Maxwell house, Mrs. Maxwell asked the men to cut Brushy loose from Rudabaugh so he could go into another room with her daughter. They refused to do it. They suspected it was a trap to allow Brushy to escape. Brushy knew if they had let him in the other room that they would go back to Garrett without him. He knew that he would find shooting irons in that room and he knew that he would be able to use them.

They started for Las Vegas, where they reached a couple of days later. Brushy almost got away from them at the jail in Las Vegas.

*Most historians agree with the following sequence of events. On December 24, the posse and their prisoners left Fort Sumner and headed north towards Las Vegas. Around midnight they reached the ranch of John Gerhardt where they spent the night. On the morning of December 25, they left for Puerto de Luna.*

*That afternoon, the posse and their prisoners arrived at Puerto de Luna where Alexander Grzelachowski cooked them a Christmas dinner. Following the meal, the posse and their prisoners continued to ride north toward Las Vegas.*

*In the late morning of December 26, the Garrett posse arrived in Las Vegas. The streets were packed with townsfolk trying to get a glimpse of the infamous prisoners and the men that captured them. The posse took the four outlaws to the town jail where they were thrown into the same cell still in shackles.*

*Brushy never mentioned these stops. It's also curious that Brushy didn't mention the "Indian servant" by name. Her name was Deluvina Maxwell. By all accounts, and in particular her own, she and Bonney were very good friends. I am sure that Bonney would have remembered her as a little bit more than just Mrs. Maxwell's "Indian servant". And I suspect that Bonney would have remembered Mrs. Maxwell's given name as well – Luz.*

The next day, they put Brushy and two of his other men on a train for Santa Fe. It looked very much like problems with a mob before they left there. At Santa Fe, they were put in jail. Brushy wrote Governor Wallace to come and talk to him, but Governor Wallace never showed up. Marshal Sherman would not let Brushy's friends visit him in jail, but he did let curiosity seekers in to see him as if he were a dog. Brushy felt that the governor had forgotten his promise to him. They took Brushy to Mesilla the last of March to stand trial on his indictments. They left Santa Fe on the train and wound up in Mesilla on a stage.

*History shows that, they arrived at Santa Fe on the evening of December 27 and were met by Deputy U. S. Marshal Charles Conklin. He accompanied Garrett's men and the prisoners to the local jail. There, they were turned over to U. S. Marshal John Sherman.*

*From his jail cell on January 1, 1881, Bonney wrote a short letter to Governor Wallace asking him to visit him in jail if he had time. Bonney was unaware that Wallace was then in Washington, D. C.*

*On March 2, Bonney wrote a second letter to Governor Wallace, not knowing he was in Silver City. In this letter, Bonney asked Wallace to visit him and hinted at blackmailing him by letting the press see the correspondence between them from back in 1879.*

*On March 4, Bonney wrote Wallace a third letter since he had not received a response from him. In this letter, Bonney reminded the governor of their bargain and that he had completely fulfilled his end, while Wallace had not. Bonney also complained of the way Marshal Sherman was treating him and of the way he was apparently being railroaded.*

*On March 27, Bonney wrote his fourth and final letter to Wallace, and pleaded to him to keep his promise. Wallace never bothered to respond.*

*On March 28, Bonney and Billy Wilson were loaded onto a train that would take them to La Mesilla for their respective trials. They were escorted by Deputy Marshals Tony Neis, Francisco Chavez, and Bonney's hated enemy, Bob Olinger. Also, riding with them was Ira Leonard who was once again acting as lawyer for Bonney.*

*Bonney wrote four letters to Governor Wallace while he was in the Santa Fe jail. Brushy mentioned only one letter. Brushy also failed to mention that they took both he and Billy Wilson to La Mesilla for trial.*

In April, Brushy pleaded to the federal indictment for killing Buckshot Roberts, and it was thrown out. Judge Leonard represented Brushy on this indictment. He got it thrown out. Brushy was then put on trial for the murder of Sheriff Brady, a territorial charge.

Again, Brushy was treated like a dog. They took him in court every morning chained and handcuffed. Olinger was there as a U. S. Deputy Marshal. He taunted and threatened Brushy continuously. Brushy tried for a six-shooter on one of the guards one day, but he couldn't quite reach it. Brushy would probably have killed Olinger first if he could have reached it.

They sat Brushy up front near old Judge Bristol, who Brushy had threatened to kill before. The judge was scared the whole time Brushy was in court in Lincoln and Mesilla. He knew that he was looking at a six-foot grave if Brushy got loose.

Judge Fountain was appointed to represent Brushy on the territorial charge. He did all he could for Brushy. Brushy had no money and couldn't get any. They didn't sell Brushy's mare up at Scott Moore's in Las Vegas. He was a friend of Brushy's, but now he said Brushy owed him for board.

Brushy felt that the trial was crooked. He asked for witnesses which they could not find because they didn't want to find them. Sheriff Garrett knew where they were. Hank Brown was in Tascosa, Texas when Brushy was on trial. Garrett knew it, too, but he didn't do anything about it.

The trial lasted about a week. The jury found Brushy guilty of the murder of Sheriff Brady, and Judge Bristol sentenced him, on April 13, to hang on May 13, in Lincoln County.

*Bonney's trial started on April 8, and the next day, April 9, he was found guilty of murdering Sheriff Brady. On April 13, he was sentenced to hang in Lincoln on May 13. Brushy said the trial last about a week, when in reality, it lasted a couple of days.*

# CHAPTER 5
## BRUSHY'S STORY
## HIS ESCAPE FROM CERTAIN DEATH

It took about five days to make the trip to Fort Stanton, where Garrett picked Brushy up and took him to the jail in Lincoln. At the Lincoln jail, Deputy U. S. Marshal Bob Olinger and James W. Bell were assigned to guard Brushy. Bell was always nice and courteous to Brushy, but Olinger was always harassing him. One morning, Olinger snarled at Brushy as usual and said, "Kid, do you see the buckshot I am loading into these two barrels, twelve in each barrel? Well, if you try to make a break, I'll put all twenty-four between your shoulder blades." Brushy replied, "Bob, you might get them before I do," and he smiled at Olinger. Olinger brought out a lariat rope and said, "This is good enough to hang you with." Brushy told him a lariat rope was not fit to hang a man with.

At noon time, as usual, Olinger went across the street with the other prisoners for lunch and left Bell there guarding Brushy. Olinger and Bell were always on guard duty. Olinger always brought Brushy a lunch when he came back. Then, Bell would go for lunch. During the week, Brushy was kept here and guarded constantly. They were afraid that Brushy would break jail or be rescued by his friends.

Olinger meant nothing to Brushy. He was a big bluff and a big coward. He killed all his men by shooting them in the back or before they knew what was happening. He was a big fellow, too. Garrett didn't like him, either.

Olinger had worked for Chisum and was not liked by any of his boys. He had shot John Jones in the back in a camp on the Pecos. Brushy had promised the father that he would even the score with Olinger for this murder of his son. During Brushy's trial at Melissa, he kept taunting and teasing Brushy. Brushy was eager to kill Olinger, but he did not want to kill Bell.

The day before, Sam Corbet and his wife came in to visit Brushy. Sam had hid a six-shooter in the outhouse. So the next morning, Brushy planned to wait until Olinger took the other prisoners to lunch and Bell would be alone with him, when he would ask Bell to take him to the outhouse. Brushy expected Bell to take him to the outhouse and he would come out shooting. But, as it turned out, Brushy didn't need Sam's six-shooter.

*According to reliable sources, Olinger escorted five other prisoners across the street to Wortley Hotel for dinner around 5 PM, leaving Bell in charge of Bonney. Shortly thereafter, Bonney asked to be taken out back to the privy. Bell unchained Bonney from the floor, though his wrists and ankles were still shackled, and led him down the stairs and out the back door to the privy. A few minutes later, Bonney emerged and walked back to the courthouse with Bell following close behind.*

*Again, it would seem Brushy's memory has failed him. On this occasion it's a question of night versus day. Olinger took the prisoners to dinner about 5 PM, not to lunch at noon as Brushy claimed. As you will read below, it was at least another hour before Bonney fled Lincoln. It was April so darkness was approaching. Wouldn't Brushy have remembered the sun setting as he left town and that the ensuing darkness had helped him slip out of the area without being detected? He fled to the west. The sun set right in front of him. How could he have missed it? This was an important event in his life. It would have been impossible for him to forget that most of his flight had been under the cover of darkness. This suggests that Brushy had only read about the escape. He just forgot reading the part about 5PM and dinner.*

Olinger is at lunch. Bell and Brushy are alone in the building. Brushy is sitting on a box, handcuffed, shackled, and chained to the floor with a lock. Bell is sitting by a window and reading a newspaper. Brushy asked Bell to unlock the chain and take him to the outhouse. At first, Bell objected; said he didn't know. Then he went into Garrett's office and got the key to unlock the chain. At this moment, Brushy slipped his right hand from the cuff and holding them with his left, he hit Bell in the back of the head. Bell tumbled over on the floor, and he was looking down the barrel of his own six-shooter.

Brushy told Bell that he would not hurt him if he would do as he said. Brushy told him to walk through the office and unlock the armory door as he wanted to lock Bell in there until he could escape. When Bell stepped into the hall, he ran for the stairway. With the fourteen-inch chain between his leg irons, Brushy could not run, so he jumped and slid across the floor to the left toward the steps. When Bell reached the third or fourth step, Brushy's left hand was nearing the stairs. Brushy pulled the trigger and the bullet struck the wall on that side. It must have ricocheted and struck Bell under the arm, coming out on the other side. Bell fell down the steps, dying as he fell.

Brushy turned and scuttled back to the office, where he picked up Olinger's shotgun where he had stood it against the wall that morning. He went over to the window. When he looked out, he saw Olinger and another man coming over across the street toward the jail. Just as Olinger came across the street, he put his six-shooter into his scabbard. He probably thought that Bell had killed Brushy in the jail. As Olinger came near the corner of the building, he passed beneath the window where Brushy was and Brushy leveled down on him, saying, "Look up, Bob. I want to shoot you in the face with your own buckshot. I don't want to shoot you in the back like you did other men, and the Jones boy." The buckshot struck him in the breast, killing him instantly. Then Brushy fired the other twelve into him. Brushy wanted Olinger to get all of them like he had promised to give them to him. Brushy wanted Olinger to know that he was the man that was killing him.

This was the happiest day of Brushy's life. He promised to give Olinger his own buckshot while Olinger was loading the gun that morning. Olinger shot the Jones boy in the back of the neck, killing him. Olinger had threatened to put the shot from both barrels in Brushy's back, and he would have done it if he would have had the chance. That was his way of killing other men, but he did not die that way.

Brushy went downstairs and out the side door at the bottom of the stairs, where old man Goss and someone else were standing near Bell's body. Brushy asked Goss to cut the chain that was between his legs. Goss tried to cut it with a saw. Brushy told him to get the axe and cut it. "And be darn careful where you hit that chain," Brushy said as he held a .44 on Goss. Goss cut the chain as Brushy stood over a rock. Brushy took a cord and tied each end of the chain to his belt so that he could straddle a horse. Goss caught a horse behind the jail in the pasture. He and the Gallegos boy saddled the horse and took it to the front of the jail. Brushy went back upstairs to the armory room and picked up a .44 Winchester belt loaded with cartridges and crossed it over his other shoulder, picking up a Winchester and two .44 single-action Colts with scabbards.

Brushy walked out on the balcony and everything was calm with no one trying to catch him. No one wanted to fight. Brushy called out to everyone and told them if anyone was looking for a six-foot grave, they should follow him.

Brushy went back downstairs and out the front of the jail, where the horse was tied. He jumped for the saddle, but slid off the other side, hanging to the rope. The Gallegos kid went down the road and took a rope off a yoke of steers in the field and tied it to Brushy's saddle.

*Although there were no other witnesses to the activities that took place within the courthouse, the following is the generally accepted version.*

*After both men were in the courthouse (See Appendix Q) two shots were fired. Bell staggered back out the door with a bullet hole in his abdomen. Hearing the shots, caretaker Godfrey Gauss, former cook at the Tunstall ranch, ran into the yard and Bell collapsed into his arms. Across the street, Olinger also heard the shots and came running, assuming that it was Bell who had shot Bonney.*

*Back in the courthouse, Bonney, on the second floor, slipped off his wrist irons, and broke into the armory, where he grabbed Olinger's brand new shotgun. Going as fast as his ankle shackles would allow, Bonney made his way back to his cell and positioned himself in the window overlooking the street. As Olinger entered the yard, Gauss yelled out to him that Bell had been killed. Olinger then heard Bonney yell out a cheerful 'Hello, Bob!' and he looked up to see his former prisoner staring down at him from the window. Bonney then fired both barrels of the shotgun. The buckshot hit the brutish deputy in the face, shoulders, and chest, killing him instantly. Next, Bonney smashed the shotgun over the window sill, breaking it at the stock, and threw it at Olinger's pulverized body, cursing Olinger.*

*As a crowd gathered in the street below, Bonney retreated inside the building and reentered the armory, where he grabbed two pistols, a Winchester rifle, and two belts of ammunition. Bonney then stepped out onto the second story balcony and addressed the crowd, telling them that he had not meant to kill Bell, but that he had been left with no other choice. He also told them that he would leave town as soon as possible.*

*Bonney then shouted to Gauss and told him to get a horse ready for him. Before going to get a horse, Gauss tossed a prospector's pick up to Bonney so that he could pry off his ankle shackles. After about an hour, Bonney finally managed to free one ankle. He then took a piece of string and tied the dangling shackle to his belt.*

*Bonney grabbed his weapons and ammunition, walked outside, and mounted the horse that Gauss had gotten for him. The horse was owned by County Clerk Billy Burt. Spooked by the loose leg iron, the horse bucked Bonney to the ground and took off down the street. Pulling his pistol, Bonney aimed it at one of the prisoners Olinger had taken to the Wortley, and ordered him to retrieve the horse. As Bonney mounted it, he said goodbye to the townsfolk, and told them to tell Burt that he would return the horse.*

*Contrast the two versions of the Olinger shooting you have just read. According to the generally accepted version, Bonney yelled out a cheerful 'Hello, Bob!' and then fired both barrels of the shotgun killing Olinger instantly. Did it happen exactly this way? Who knows, but at least it's believable. Brushy's account is quite different. Rather than a simple 'Hello, Bob', Brushy said he greeted Olinger with: "Look up, Bob. I want to shoot you in the face with your own buckshot. I don't want to shoot you in the back like you did other men, and the Jones boy." Brushy would have you believe he gave a speech while Olinger waited patiently in the street below. Believable? Not hardly!*

Brushy got on the horse and rode out of Lincoln to the west and up a canyon to the home of a friend, who cut the bolts in his leg irons. After they screwed the nuts on the bolts, they riveted over the ends of the bolts so Brushy couldn't unscrew them with his hands.

Brushy turned the horse back for Lincoln and walked over the mountain. His guns began to get heavy and he hung one of them in the fork of a tree. Brushy was headed for the house of Higinio Salazar. They had been friends for a long time. Brushy had stayed with him and his mother before. Neither of them was married. Brushy could reach Salazar's house across the mountain and Salazar would help him as much as he could.

Higinio was the one who escaped from the burning McSween building. He was seriously injured, but he recovered. Brushy walked near the house and whistled several times before he came outside. Salazar recognized him and they talked about Brushy's escape. He urged me to leave for Old Mexico. Brushy argued that he would not leave until he killed John Chisum, Barney Mason, and Garrett. Salazar went back in the house and brought a blanket for Brushy. Brushy slept in the underbrush, as he thought a posse would be looking for him.

The next day, Salazar brought food to Brushy. On the second day, he borrowed a horse and Brushy started for Fort Sumner across the plains. Brushy told Salazar about hanging his pistol in the tree and he tried to find it, but never did.

*There are various versions of what happened after Bonney left Lincoln, but the following is the most widely accepted version.*

*From Lincoln, Bonney rode west for a short distance, then north through the canyon leading to the ranch of his friend, Juan Padilla, where he left the horse. He then took off on foot up the canyon to Jose Cordova's house a few miles west of Padilla's.*

*It is believed that Cordova and his son, Manuel, helped Bonney to remove the shackles. The shackles had rubbed his skin raw and it had started to bleed. Cordova asked Bonney to stay overnight and rest up so that he could minister to his wounds. Bonney said that he needed to get to Yginio's as soon as possible; besides a posse was probably not too far behind.*

*Late that night, Bonney arrived at the house of his friend Yginio Salazar near Las Tablas at the base of the Capitans and spent a few days with Salazar. Salazar got a horse for Bonney that belonged to Andrew Richardson at the Three Block ranch. The horse was part mustang and quarter horse, swift and of great endurance, and just the animal needed to put space between Bonney and any pursuers.*

*Brushy never went into much detail as to how he got the leg irons off, nor did he identify any of the people who helped him flee after his escape. Those would seem to be some more rather important details that Brushy has again forgotten.*

While on his way to Fort Sumner, the horse broke loose and Brushy was on foot again. He walked into Anaya's sheep camp below Fort Sumner and stayed a few days. Brushy traveled at night and slept during the daytime. He suspected that Garrett was at Fort Sumner hunting for him. After dark one evening, he walked to the home of Charlie Bowdre's widow, where he spent the night, and the next day or so. From here, Brushy rode back to Garcia's. He stayed around Fort Sumner with some ranchers and herders for about two and a half months before he had the fight with Garrett's posse that night in July. He would not leave until he had killed Chisum, Barney Mason, and Garrett.

*Most historians agree that the following sequence of events occurred: On May 1, Bonney left Salazar's house on his new horse that his friend had gotten him and headed south, probably in an attempt to lead any pursuing posses on a wild goose chase. He soon arrived at the ranch of friend John Meadows. Meadows and Tom Norris had a cabin on the Rio Penasco at the time and had not heard of Bonney's escape.*

*Meadows advised Bonney to ride to Mexico, but Bonney refused, saying he was going to head north towards Fort Sumner. Why Bonney wanted to return to Fort Sumner is a mystery. The most logical thing for him to have done, would have been to flee the territory altogether. Maybe he was going back for a girlfriend, or maybe to be with friends, or maybe he thought it would be the one place pursuers would not suspect him to be. Or, maybe it was to plan his revenge on Pat Garrett, Barney Mason, and John Chisum.*

*On May 7, Bonney walked into Fort Sumner. His horse had gotten away from him. He stayed with various friends in town. Rumors soon reached Garrett in Lincoln that Bonney was around Fort Sumner, but he dismissed them, believing that Bonney was far from New Mexico.*

About the middle of May, 1881, Brushy rode out to John Chisum's ranch on South Spring. He met a Mexican cowboy. He pulled down on the Mexican, telling him to go in and bring Old John out so he could talk to him in his language. The Mexican told him that Old John had left the country when Brushy broke out of jail over in Lincoln, and that he would not come back. Brushy threatened to kill the Mexican if Old John didn't come out. The Mexican kept insisting that Old John was not in there. Brushy promised the Mexican that he would kill him if he found out that he is lying to him. Brushy stayed at a camp nearby for a few days watching and waiting until he found out the Mexican was telling the truth.

Brushy left there looking for Barney Mason. Barney started to ride up to the camp where Brushy was staying. By the time Brushy came out, Barney had left, and in a mighty hurry. Brushy could have killed him if he had known it was him.

Brushy sent a note to Garrett telling him that he was waiting for him, and that he had better show up shooting, too. Barney and Pat had both been good friends of Brushy's until Chisum and others had Garrett elected sheriff of Lincoln County. They rode and gambled together. Mason rustled cattle and horses with Brushy and his friends after Garrett was elected. But, when Barney started squealing to Garrett, they ran him off.

*Brushy said that he sent a note to Garrett telling him that, "he was waiting for him, so he had better show up shooting?" That's very doubtful. History states that Garrett never knew where Bonney was until the day he shot and killed him. If Brushy had written a note to Garrett telling him he was waiting for him, that implies that Garrett knew where Brushy was, and that Brushy knew it. If Garrett had known where Brushy was, why did it take so long to pay him a visit? And if Brushy had even suspected that Garrett knew his location, wouldn't he have gone somewhere else? The more you read, the more you see why Brushy could not have been Billy the Kid. Or could he? He was old, and time had obviously taken its toll on his memory. Maybe he was just embellishing the story a bit?*

Celsa and Pat's wife were sisters to Saval Gutierrez. Celsa was one of Brushy's sweethearts when he was in Fort Sumner. Her brother, Saval, lived in Fort Sumner. After Brushy returned from hunting Old John, Saval went up to Canaditas and got Celsa for him, but Brushy did not want to get married until Garrett was gone.

*Celsa was in fact a sister of Apolonaria, the wife of Pat Garrett. They were daughters of Jose Delores Gutierrez. However, Celsa was not Saval Gutierrez's sister; she was his wife! In the census on Jun 14, 1880, Sabal (Saval) Gutierrez and Celsa were listed as husband and wife with a three year old daughter Mauricia. On that day, their home was recorded in Fort Sumner three dwellings away from the Maxwells. If we are to believe Brushy, Saval Gutierrez went up to Canaditas and fetched his wife for Brushy. What a friend! And Brushy said he "did not want to get married until Garrett was gone"? If Brushy had wanted to marry Celsa, the person who had to go wasn't Garrett; it was Celsa's husband, Saval. In fairness to Brushy, it's easy to understand his confusion. Who wouldn't be confused? After all, Celsa was a Gutierrez before she married a Gutierrez. Such marriages have confused many a "reader". But this one should not have confused Brushy – not if he had been there. If he had been there, wouldn't he have remembered that his sweetheart was already married? He was in their house, he remembered both of them, but he remembered them as brother and sister! How is that possible? It's not; not if he were there.*

While Brushy was in Fort Sumner, he stayed at Gutierrez's, Jesus Silva's, and Bowdre's. He also stayed at the Yerby ranch north of Fort Sumner quite a bit. They were good friends. Brushy kept horses and mules when Charlie Bowdre worked for Yerby. Yerby had a good-looking daughter, who was sort of a sweetheart of Brushy's. Fort Sumner had some good-looking girls in those days.

*Brushy really should have kept his love life out of his story. Here he has claimed Yerby's daughter as another of his sweethearts. Thomas Yerby did have a daughter, but she was only two years old when Brushy staked his claim to her. On June 16, when the 1880 census was taken, the only daughter listed for 30 year old Tomas (Thomas) Yerby and his 18 year old mistress/companion, Nasaria, was Florentina , age two. A son,*

*Juan, age three, was also listed in this household. Florentina may have been good looking and she may have been a sweetheart, but she certainly wasn't Brushy's sweetheart. Brushy, of course was not referring to Florentina; he must have been referring to Nasaria. He had simply forgotten her name. And he didn't know that Nasaria was Yerby's mistress; that wasn't part of the story that Brushy had read or heard. The story that Brushy remembered depicted Nasaria as the daughter of Thomas Yerby. Some versions of it have even portrayed Florentina as the daughter of Nasaria and Billy the Kid. This story of course is nothing more than completely unsubstantiated lore and is not taken seriously by any reputable historian. Just for the sake of argument, what if it was true, would it support Brushy's story? Well, if it was true, and Brushy was Billy the Kid, it would mean that Brushy had not only forgotten to mention the only child he ever fathered, but had also forgotten the name of that child's mother! It is much more likely that Brushy was only recalling this lore when he mentioned that Yerby's daughter was another of his sweethearts. He just forgot the part about him being a father.*

# CHAPTER 6
## BRUSHY'S STORY
## A DEATH AT FORT SUMNER AND THE AFTER LIFE

Brushy rode into Fort Sumner from Yerby's a few days before Garrett and his posse rode in. When they rode in that day, Brushy spent the day with Garrett's brother-in-law, Saval Gutierrez. Nearly all the people in this country were friends of Brushy's and they helped him. None of them liked Garrett.

*Remember that "Garrett's brother-in-law, Saval Gutierrez" as Brushy described him here, was really the brother-in-law of Pat Garrett's wife Apolonaria. Saval Gutierrez was married to Apolonaria's older sister Celsa. This the same Celsa that Brushy remembered as his sweetheart and as Saval's sister. Confusing? Yes, but it wouldn't have been for someone who had actually been there and who had known these folks.*

Garrett and his posse came in that night while Brushy and his friends were at a dance. Silva saw Garrett in Fort Sumner a little while before Brushy and his friends rode into town from the dance. He knew that Brushy was staying with Gutierrez, so he went over there to warn him to leave town. Gutierrez told him that they were out to a dance.

When Brushy, his partner, and the girls rode into town, they stopped at Jesus Silva's. Jesus told Celsa that Garrett was in town looking for Brushy. About midnight, the girls left and Brushy began asking about Garrett. Silva got excited and told them to leave before Garrett found them there. Brushy thought Garrett would go to Gutierrez's and he had better stay away that night. He told Silva that they were not going until they had something to eat. Silva agreed to fix a meal for them.

Silva was cooking the meal for them to eat when Brushy's partner asked for fresh beef. Silva said that if one of them would go over to Maxwell's and get some beef he would cook it for them. Brushy sensed a trap, but his partner insisted that they go get the beef. His partner started out to Maxwell's after Brushy refused to leave Silva's house. He thought that Garrett might still be in town, and he wanted to meet him in the daytime so he could beat him to the draw.

*Let's review what Brushy has just told us. Brushy had just left Thomas Yerby's home where Brushy had visited his sweetheart, Yerby's daughter. Again, he has mistaken Yerby's mistress, Nasaria, for Yerby's daughter.*

*When Brushy arrived in Fort Sumner, he spent the day with Saval Gutierrez and his wife Celsa, whom Brushy mistakenly believed to have been another of his sweethearts. In fact, according to Brushy, his good friend Saval Gutierrez had gone up to Canaditas and fetched Celsa (his own wife) for him. Now Brushy tells us that he and his friends were at a dance that evening when Garrett and his posse rode into town. Among those friends would have been Celsa and the fellow Brushy will soon introduce to us as "his partner".*

*According to Brushy, Jesus Silva saw Garrett in town and went to Saval Gutierrez to warn Brushy. Brushy of course was not there since he was out dancing with "his partner" and Saval's wife Celsa. Jesus Silva, apparently not wanting to put a damper on Brushy's fun evening, went back home rather than going to the dance to warn Brushy.*

*After the dance, "Brushy, his partner, and the girls rode into town" and stopped at Jesus Silva's. Here we meet Brushy's partner for the first time - and none to soon, for he has but a short time to live. Jesus Silva then told Celsa that Garrett was in town looking for Brushy. Why didn't Jesus tell Brushy himself? Was he embarrassed that he hadn't ridden out to the dance to warn him earlier?*

*Brushy said the girls left Silva's about midnight. After all, Celsa had a husband and daughter at home waiting for her! Now Brushy had a hunger attack. Jesus Silva agreed to fix them a meal, but Brushy's "partner" wanted fresh beef. Jesus pointed them to Maxwell's. So Brushy's partner headed off to Maxwell's (See Appendix S) for fresh beef and his date with destiny. Brushy remained behind because he wanted to meet Garrett "in the daytime so he could beat him to the draw". Does anybody believe any of this? Consider the following excerpt from an interview given in 1937 by Jesus Silva to Jack Hull:*

*"It was the night of July 14, 1881. It had been a hot day throughout the valley and Mesa Redondo country. I had strolled over to a neighbor's house and on my return had stopped under a Cottonwood tree for a moment, when the Kid, whom I had known for some time, strolled up. He had just ridden into town. He was hot and tired and we drank beer together. He told me he was hungry and that he was going to the home of Don Pedro Maxwell for a cut of fresh beef for his supper, which was being prepared at a nearby house. We parted there and in a few minutes there were shots. The news soon spread that Garrett had shot the Kid at Maxwell's home. I ran over there and Garrett, who had run out of the house, told me to go in and see if the Kid was dead."*

*Do you think that just maybe Brushy had read the same interview? He remembered the "fresh beef". He just forgot the part about it having happened under a cottonwood tree and not in Silva's house. He also forgot that it was he who went "to the home of Don Pedro Maxwell for a cut of fresh beef." Of course that wouldn't fit Brushy's story since that fellow, Brushy's "partner", was shot dead, placed in a box made by Jesus Silva and buried in a grave dug by Jesus Silva and Vicente Otero.*

In a short time, they heard pistol shots. Brushy ran through the gate into Maxwell's back yard in the bright moonlight and started shooting at the shadows along the house. One of their first shots had killed his partner on the back porch. After entering the yard, their first shot struck Brushy in the lower jaw, taking out a tooth as it went through his mouth. As he started over the back fence, another shot struck him in the back of his left shoulder. Brushy had emptied one of his .44's when another shot struck him across the top of his head about an inch and a half back of his forehead and about two inches in length. This shot knocked him out and he stumbled into the gallery of an adobe behind Maxwell's yard fence. A Mexican woman was living there, and she pulled him in through the door. When Brushy woke up, she was putting beef tallow on his head to stop the flow of blood. Brushy told her to reload his .44's which she did.

*A shot knocked Brushy out and he stumbled into the gallery of an adobe behind Maxwell's yard fence? This was a remarkable feat indeed. Not only did Brushy stumble into the gallery after having been knocked out, but he remembered doing it.*

*As history has it, inside the bedroom, Garrett had awakened Maxwell and was sitting at the head of the bed asking Maxwell if he knew where Bonney was. Garrett then saw a figure enter the bedroom who asked Maxwell, in Spanish, who the men on the porch were. Recognizing the voice of Bonney, Garrett drew his pistol and fired two quick shots before he and Maxwell ran out of the room.*

*In all that has been written of the events on this fateful night in Fort Sumner, none have recorded more than two shots being fired. Nor, has there ever been any mention of Garrett and his men shooting at another person trying to escape.*

*Up to this point Brushy has had a script to guide him – the stories he had read and the stories he had heard. Now he is on his own. From this point forward, Brushy will be winging it. As you will see, Brushy may have been a lot of things, but he was no eagle. Also note here that Brushy said one of their first shots had killed "his partner" on the back porch. Can't Brushy remember his name?*

Brushy started to go back out after them when Celsa came running in and said that they had killed his partner, Barlow, and that they were passing his body off as his. She begged Brushy to leave town. She said that they would not leave Maxwell's house for the night. They were afraid of being mobbed.

About 3 o'clock in the morning, Celsa brought Brushy's horse up to the adobe. He pushed his .44's into the scabbards and rode out of town with Frank Lobato. They stayed at the sheep camp the next day. Then Brushy moved to another camp south of Fort Sumner, where he stayed until his wounds healed enough to travel.

*Brushy stated that he "started to go back out after them when Celsa came running in and said that they had killed his partner, Barlow ...'"? Who was Brushy going back out after? Was it Garrett and his posse? Remember a short time earlier Brushy had said he wanted to meet Garrett "in the daytime so he could beat him to the draw". Now wounded, he's going after Garrett and his posse in the dark? We know it's dark because he said Celsa brought him his horse at "3 o'clock in the morning". How did Celsa know where to find Brushy? And what was Celsa doing in the Maxwell house that evening? Shouldn't she have been home with her husband and their daughter? Why would Celsa have been afraid of being mobbed? She was Brushy's sweetheart and the mob thought it was Brushy who had been killed.*

*Whatever the case, it's fortunate that Brushy thought Celsa was there since it was through her that he finally identified his "partner" as Barlow. This was undoubtedly the "Billy Barlow" for whom there has never been found a shred of evidence that he ever existed. Morrison interviewed Brushy and wrote his story. Wouldn't Morrison have pressed*

*Brushy for a little more information on his "partner's" identity? This was the guy whose body was supposedly passed off as Brushy's. His identity was critical. Even a lawyer would have understood that.*

About the first of August, Brushy started for El Paso, where he had lots of friends. He crossed the Rio Grande north of town and went into Sonora, Mexico, where he was acquainted with the Yaqui Indians. He lived with them nearly two years.

In the fall of 1882, Brushy left Mexico and went to Grand Saline, Texas. He was dressed like an Indian and he took a job driving a wagon from there to Carlton, Texas, where his folks had lived. He hoped to find them there. He made two trips hauling salt, but never found his folks.

*Brushy previously said that he lived with the Yaqui Indians in Mexico for almost two years. Now, he says that he is in Grand Saline after only one year. As you have seen, and will see as you read further, Brushy's story becomes less and less believable.*

He went back to Sonora, Mexico, where he stayed until the winter of 1883. At that time, he returned to Texas as the Texas Kid. He worked a short time at the Powers Cattle Company. From there, he went up to Decatur, Texas, where he struck up again with Indian Jim. He had worked with Jim in No Man's Land in 1875 and again in Arizona on the Gila Ranch in the spring of 1877.

*Henry McCarty was jailed in Silver City, New Mexico on September 23, 1875 for stealing clothes from a Chinese laundry. A couple of days later, he escaped and went directly to the house of his family's good friends, the Truesdells. Mrs. Truesdell gave him some Chauncey's clothes and sent him up to Ed Moulton's sawmill at Bear Mountain. Chauncey was one of Henry's childhood friends and Ed Moulton had been a family friend.*

*A few days later, Henry returned to the Truesdell home and one morning, Mrs. Truesdell gave him all the money she had and put him on a stage to Globe, Arizona (see Appendix P). She was hoping that Henry would find William Antrim, 'his stepfather', and stay with him. It has been written by some that Henry found William, but William told him to leave after being told of his troubles.*

*Henry was not in No Man's Land in 1875. He left Silver City in late September or early October, 1875 and went straight to Arizona. He could not have worked with an Indian Jim in No Man's Land in 1875.*

While on a cattle drive in Kansas City, Brushy was arrested and held by the law as being Billy the Kid. The boys got him off though.

*How were the lawmen in Kansas City able to mistakenly identify Brushy as Billy the Kid? Billy the Kid had been 'killed' earlier in Fort Sumner, New Mexico and they would surely have known that; it was in all the newspapers. Furthermore, there were no official photographs of Bonney circulating at that time, nor were there were any 'wanted' posters. As far as the law was concerned, the case was closed. Billy the Kid was dead.*

Then Indian Jim and Brushy went to work for Tom Waggoner, at Decatur, breaking horses. Late in the winter, they left for the Black Hills of Dakota. They joined the scouts, guarding the stage lines on the Idaho Trail. They stayed with the scouts for about three or four years. During this time, he earned the name of Brushy Bill from riding in the brushy hills of the Dakotas.

Often times, they stopped in Cold Creek, Idaho, where Brushy joined the Missionary Baptist Church. Those were tough times, but during those days, he defied any man to beat him to the draw. While working on the scout gang, Brushy rode for Buffalo Bill on his ranch at North Platte, Nebraska. It was here where he later on rode the Black Diamond mare in open prairie. No one else had ridden her in the open before.

In the spring of 1888, Brushy joined the Pinkerton detectives. That fall, he joined the Anti-Horse Thief Association to clear Texas of horse thieves. They rode up and down the Red River, in east Texas, and in Indian Territory. They rode up the Ozark Trail in Missouri before they quit. Brushy investigated many cases of counter branding. Several times, with some quick shooting, Brushy shot the branding iron from the hands of the thief.

*"Several times, with some quick shooting, Brushy shot the branding iron from the hands of the thief". Does anybody really believe that "Brushy shot the branding iron from the hands of the thief"? And not just once, but several times! Why would anybody shoot a branding iron? Wouldn't the thief have been a better target? Bonney and anybody else, who wanted to live to shoot another day, would have shot the rustler, not the branding iron. That's the stuff of movies and dime store novels, not reality.*

Judge Parker, a United States Judge at Fort Smith, Arkansas, asked

Brushy to go into the Ozark Mountains to pick up the many gangs of thieves operating there. He offered him twenty-five men. Brushy refused, telling the judge, "Those men know their hills and hideouts too well." Brushy told him it would be suicide, but to wait until spring when the thieves came out of hiding with their stolen horses. It took them four years to break the gangs up. All the offenses committed in Indian Territory were tried by Old Judge Parker at Fort Smith. Brushy was well acquainted with Judge Parker.

*Are we really to believe that Brushy went from rustler and legendary outlaw to law enforcement agent? Why would he take a chance of being identified by the other lawmen with whom he worked? Brushy just told us of his arrest as Billy the Kid while on a cattle drive in Kansas City. Now he's hanging out with the law on a regular basis? And Brushy says he was well acquainted with Judge Parker? The last person on Earth with whom Bonney would have become well acquainted would have been Judge Parker. He was called the "hanging judge" for good reason and Bonney would have known it. Judge Parker would never have been counted in Bonney's circle of close acquaintances, nor would any other law enforcement officials.*

While going over to the Creek Nation to Round Top Mountain in 1888, Brushy and his friends were invited to a big dance, to which they went. They were looking for stolen horses. It was a regular outlaw dance and Brushy would call it. A fight started that night. Al Jennings and some others rode out. Four men were killed and seven others were wounded. When the shooting started in the house, Brushy could see that he couldn't get out, so he just lied down on the floor. About the time the shooting ceased, a man came in and turned Brushy over, saying, "Did I get you, Tony? If I knew I didn't, I'd finish you up." Brushy said nothing and played dead. The man thought that Brushy was Tony McClure, a deputy marshal.

Brushy got up and went out of the house and started to get some water from the well, running over two wounded men. The first thing a wounded man wants is water. So, Brushy went to the well and filled his hat with water. He began to give it to them. Jack Shaw, Tony McClure, and Ozark Jack were all shot up pretty bad. They went down to the ravine, got their horses, and pulled back to the Chickasaw Nation.

Brushy joined the U. S. Marshal's force in 1892. During that time he was a deputy marshal, he saw six train holdups. He and his fellow officers saved three of them from losing money. The Daltons held up a train in the spring of 1892. They killed a deputy who failed to put his hands up fast enough. One of them looked at Brushy and said, "We know who you are. Put 'em up or I'll kill you." When the judge asked why they let the Daltons get away, Brushy told him that he knew the Daltons and he didn't want to fight them alone either. "They all put up their hands except one man, and he is buried out there, too".

*Does this story sound a little fishy? "We know who you are. Put them up or I'll kill you." How could they possibly have known that Brushy was Billy the Kid? Or, maybe they thought he was Jesse James?*

"Cherokee Bill's gang held up a train. Joe Shaw's boys got one, too. Joe was a good safe-cracker. They didn't get anything. Al Jennings held up a train. They didn't get much. There were four bank holdups and we saved two of them".

Brushy was with the bunch that took Robber's Roost. Also, he was in the bunch that captured Crazy Snake, the Indian. Brushy and his men chased them into the mountains, where they hid. Their boys brought food to them. A marshal named Jones roped one of the boys and hung him to a tree till he was glad to tell Brushy and his men where the Indians were hiding. After a brief trial, the court turned them loose.

In the fall of 1888, there was a cowboy roundup staged in Cheyenne, Wyoming. The judges wanted Brushy to enter the contest riding a horse known as Cyclone. Brushy didn't have the entry fee. He rode horses of every make, breed, and color on every ranch in the state till he was really saddle toughened. Then, he knew he was ready for old Cyclone. So, in 1889, He returned to the roundup. Tom Waggoner covered all bets and Brushy won the championship riding Cyclone, and Tom gave him $10,000 for winning for him. Brushy was known as the Hugo Kid.

Brushy and Indian Jim went to Oklahoma City for the winter. In January of 1890, Indian Jim sent Brushy to a boxing school in Cincinnati, Ohio, where he trained. Brushy was tired of riding outlaw horses and thought he would like to be a boxer. He was left-handed and fast, but they put him in the ring with a long-armed fellow, and Brushy decided that his arms were too short to continue boxing. He went back to Oklahoma City and rode horses again in his spare time. Brushy and Indian Jim kept riding the anti-horse-thief trail.

Brushy rode Crazy Fox in Old Mexico. Crazy Fox was a buckskin horse with a black stripe down his back and black stripes around his legs. He weighed about a thousand pounds and was well built, about eight years old, with a ewe neck and a Roman nose, and it looked as if both his eyes came out the same place. Brushy contested him according to Cheyenne rules. Crazy Fox pitched like a mountain horse, only worse while it lasted, but not so long. Pitching about 300 yards, he broke into a run. Jim roped him, and they didn't want to pay off. They finally paid up, and Brushy and Indian Jim went to Fort Worth, Texas.

*Wait just a minute. Brushy said that he went to work for Judge Parker in 1888 and worked for him four years. In 1889, he returned to work for Tom Waggoner at Decatur, Texas and then he went to Cheyenne, Wyoming and rode 'Cyclone'. Then in 1890, he went to a boxing school in Cincinnati, Ohio. Brushy surely had the fastest horse in the West.*

After that, Brushy went to Sulphur Springs, Texas, where he rode Lone Wolf in Booger Red's show. They went on to Cold Creek, Idaho, where he rode Wild Cat in the summer of 1892. In the fall, he rode the Black Diamond mare at Buffalo Bill's ranch on North Platte. Then, he rode Wild Hyena at Pendleton, Oregon, Smokey at the Diamond A, and Man Killer in Cheyenne.

In 1893, Brushy's riding skills gave him a trip to the Argentine Republic. A company had shipped a large bunch of Western Horses down there. The natives couldn't do anything with them. The Cattleman's Association sent Brushy and Indian Jim there to break the horses. They left Oklahoma City about the 10th of January, 1893, and sailed to Buenos Aires. For the first few days, they looked around to see the brands on the horses so they could tell where the horses came from. They found quite a few Wyoming horses in the herd.

Brushy was supposed to ride four horses a day, two in the morning and two in the afternoon. After Brushy and Indian Jim taught the Argentines how to ride, they showed them how to drive the horses. Brushy would ride four one day and the Argentines would take them the next day, and so on. After Brushy and Indian Jim was there six months, the Argentines suggested that they have a contest ride. They held a contest for three days, riding horses and steers, and bulldogging and roping just like they did in the United States.

On the third day, Brushy rode Zebra Dan. Zebra Dan was an outlaw when he was shipped there. Brushy asked them to raise a bet and he'd ride him. He told them that he was supposed to ride him away, but he would like to have it sweetened. After Brushy stepped off, he put a bridle on him and hopped on and rode him with a bridle. Brushy had taught the Argentines to ride in the slick and to ride with a surcingle. Now, they wanted him to ride Zebra Dan with a surcingle, which he did.

*Brushy was awfully busy between 1888 and 1893. He worked for the Pinkerton detectives, rode for the Anti-Horse Thief Association, joined the U. S. Marshal's force, worked for Judge Parker in Fort Smith, Arkansas, rode bucking horses from Old Mexico to Wyoming to Oregon, went to Cincinnati, Ohio to train as a boxer, and sailed on a ship to Argentina to break horses. These tales are very similar to those he told during his Billy the Kid days in and around New Mexico when he was everywhere, sometimes in different places at the same time. In short, they are just simply not believable. Nobody could have held that many jobs in that many places in that short a period of time, not then; not even today.*

Some time in 1894, Brushy and Indian Jim contracted to go to the Shetland Islands to catch ponies. They were hard to rope in that brush. They would run like rabbits. Brushy and Indian Jim spent about three months catching some 150 head of ponies. When they came back, they joined up again with the Anti-Horse Thief Association in Indian Territory. They were put on the North Canadian River.

One morning, Brushy and Mountain Bill were riding along when a shot struck Bill from across the river. He fell off his horse, wounded. Brushy drew his rifle from the scabbard. Taking his field glasses, Brushy spied a Creek Indian across the river. He fired four shots. The Indian never showed up anymore. Brushy put Bill on his horse and took him to a cow ranch some ten miles away. They shipped Bill to Ardmore, where he died from the wound. Brushy wrote to his sister in Arizona and his brother-in-law came and got his belongings. Brushy made a report of all this and they signed him up with a fellow named Boyles.

In the fall of 1894, Brushy went back on the marshal force and served three more years. He would take off a couple of months each year and ride with Buffalo Bill's and Pawnee Bill's Wild West shows.

In 1895, Brushy struck out for El Paso, Texas, where he ran into a bunch of cowboys with whom he was acquainted. They said it was a good time to put up a ranch in Old Mexico, as Old Diaz had offered good terms for grazing land. By paying a small fee, you could graze all the land you needed. It looked like a good proposition. Ten of them, including Brushy, agreed to put up a ranch over there, with not more than ten shares to each man. They bought a thousand head of cattle and fifty ponies. They fixed up everything and appointed a boss. Brushy decided to put Indian Jim in his place and he went back to Indian Territory. Late in the fall, he went back to Old Mexico, arriving there about Christmas at the ranch. He was still called Hugo Kid there. They ranched through the years of 1896 and 1897, raising mules and steel-dust horses.

*Brushy's stories are very contradictory. He said that in the fall of 1894, he went back with the marshal force and served three more years. Yet he says in 1895, that he struck out for El Paso, where he met up with a bunch of men who set up a ranch in Old Mexico which they ranched through 1896 and 1897. Was he working undercover in Old Mexico for U. S. Marshal's force? It just doesn't add up.*

In the spring of 1898, Roosevelt called for volunteers for his regiment of Rough Riders. Jim and Brushy were in Claremore, Oklahoma about this time, so they went to Muskogee and enlisted. They were transferred to San Antonio, Texas, where they stayed about three weeks before they started for Cuba. They went through Mobile, Alabama, where they were given a midnight supper. It was not long before they landed in Cuba. A lieutenant by the name of Cook stepped up to Brushy and said, "Ain't this the Texas Kid?" Brushy told him it was, and the lieutenant said, "You'd make a good scout. You were good in Indian Territory scouting horse thieves. We will take you and the Cherokee Indian for scouts."

*It is hard to figure out which alias Brushy was going by at any given time. Brushy says Belle Starr labeled him the 'Texas Kid' while he was with her in 1874. Then he was 'Brushy Bill' while riding the brushy hills of the Dakotas around 1884 to 1887. After that he was the 'Hugo Kid' when he rode for Tom Waggoner in 1889 and he was still called the 'Hugo Kid' in 1896 and 1897 in Old Mexico. But in 1898, Lieutenant Cook of the Rough Riders recognized him as the 'Texas Kid'. How did the lieutenant know that he ever went by 'Texas Kid'? But, Brushy has some far bigger problems when it comes to his story about serving with the Rough Riders.*

*Brushy's Rough Rider story holds up only until San Antonio, Texas. After San Antonio, it's pure and utter nonsense. And that's putting it mildly. After leaving San Antonio en-route to Cuba, Brushy says "went through Mobile, Alabama, where they were given a midnight supper." It must have been a memorable supper. Following this supper, he states that "It was not long before they landed in Cuba". Brushy must have gone on alone without the rest of the Rough Riders. The real Rough Riders departed San Antonio by rail on or about 27 May 1898. They arrived in Tampa Florida on 1 June with their horses. They boarded the ship "Yucatan" in Tampa Bay on 8 June amid much confusion, and without their horses. The only horses taken aboard were those of the officers. Keep in mind, as you read more of Brushy's account, that the Rough Riders went to war as a "dismounted cavalry unit". After more delay, the Yucatan hoisted anchor and shipped out on 13 June. It was not until 22 June that the Rough Riders landed in Daiquiri, Cuba. So the trip from San Antonio to Cuba was somewhat longer and more complicated than Brushy remembered. The only real name that Brushy mentions in his Rough Rider story is Lieutenant Cook. Who was Lieutenant Cook? Who knows, but he wasn't a Rough Rider. There were four Cooks on the roster, but they were all privates. Lieutenant Cook and Billy Barlow share a common origin, Brushy's imagination.*

They would put one to fifteen on a scout gang and the scout gang would hunt the enemy out and report back to headquarters. Brushy told Jim that they had put themselves up as another target. Brushy followed that about two months, seeing scouts shot on every side of him. Jim and Brushy always made it out.

They shipped lots of Western ponies down there, and there were lots of them that the boys couldn't ride. Cook told them he could get them a man that could ride them. So, they sent for Brushy and the Indian to come down to the corral. Brushy saddled up one of the ponies and kicked him out like he had always ridden. They said that they would give Brushy a job of riding the ponies. Brushy told them he wanted Jim for a helper. He thought this was better than being shot in ambush.

In a little while, Brushy had charge of these horses. Some of the officers didn't like this and Brushy told them to take off their stripes, which they did, and Brushy and Jim proved their manhood. In about four days, Brushy whipped two of them, but still held his job. The officers treated lots of the boys mean.

*As to Brushy's "scout gang", he must be describing a different war. Brushy describes how he spent "about two months, seeing scouts shot on every side of him." Well, they landed on 22 June and the war has been described as "virtually over" with the capture of San Juan heights on 1 July. He says they "shipped lots of Western ponies down there". They didn't. He says "there were lots of them that the boys couldn't ride". Yes, there were because the boys were in Cuba and the horses were back in Tampa. Brushy says that he and Jim "proved their manhood" by whipping two officers who didn't like the idea that Brushy "had charge of these horses". Whipping a couple of officers was not a smart way to prove one's manhood, and the horses were imaginary.*

During a battle one day, there were four officers shot in the back. They thought that Brushy and the Cherokee Indian did it, which they tried to prove in a court-martial, but failed. When our time was out, they gave us a bobtailed discharge. Brushy didn't think he was entitled to it, because they did not prove anything on him.

*If four officers had been shot in the back, there would be a record of it. There is not one. If they or anyone else had been court-martialed for such an offense, there would be a record of it. There is not. Brushy is about to muster out of the Rough Riders and he still hasn't mentioned the "charge up San Juan Hill". All things considered, I think it's pretty clear that he never heard of it.*

Brushy and Indian Jim mustered out, coming back to the United States. They went back to Old Mexico on the ranch. In June, 1899, old Diaz seized everything. The Mexicans would not let Brushy and his friends ship or drive cattle out of there. They sent soldiers down to drive their stuff off. Brushy and his friends asked for thirty days grace. They thought they might get some help from the United States. If not, they could get some ammunition.

About fifty Mexican soldiers came there to round up their cattle and horses. Brushy and his friends sent an interpreter down to talk to the soldiers. They said that it was Diaz's orders. There were thirty-six cowboys in Brushy's group. The cowboys fired into the soldiers with .30-30 rifles and picked them off like blackbirds.

*Billy the Kid was fluent in Spanish and would not have needed to send interpreters to talk to the Mexican soldiers. Wouldn't he have gone himself? Apparently, Brushy did not remember any Spanish even though he had spent all those years in New Mexico, and even more recently in Old Mexico.*

The fourth morning when cowboys got up, they were surrounded by almost two thousand soldiers. Brushy climbed up on the barn and tacked up a red blanket. Each cowboy packed his horse like he was going off for a day's ride. The cowboys agreed to fire into the soldiers weakest spot, then make their getaway if they could.

They fought for twelve days, living on wild game and trying to escape into the United States. On the thirteenth morning, they crossed the Rio Grande below Del Rio, Texas. Brushy had a cousin there on the Texas Ranger force. He helped them with food. Brushy was supposed to be worth about thirty thousand dollars, but came out with one horse and one saddle.

*Brushy and 35 friends fought two thousand Mexican soldiers for 12 days without losing a man? While surrounded by these two thousand solders they were able to hunt wild game on which they lived? And they were able to escape by firing into the soldiers weakest spot? Where would that spot be in a force of two thousand soldiers encircling 36? Just think, if Brushy and his group had been at the Alamo, how different things there might have been.*

In the spring of 1902, Brushy started a Wild West show which he operated until 1904. Then he went to Canton, in Van Zandt County, Texas. From Canton, he went into Indian Territory, trading horses and cattle.

Brushy went back to Old Mexico about 1907 and three of them started another ranch known as the Three Bar. In 1910, the revolution came along, and they started fighting again. They joined with Carranza's men and later with Pancho Villa. Brushy was a captain of 106 men, all mounted on steel-dust horses from their ranch. Their steel-dust horses could outdistance the Spanish ponies of the Federals. They left Mexico in 1914, coming across the border at Brownsville, Texas. The Mexican revolution broke them up. They lost everything they had, about $200,000 between the three of them.

In 1912, Brushy met Mollie Brown of Coleman, Texas, and they were married. She was a member of the old Brown family of Brownwood, Texas. They went back to east Texas and then to Oklahoma in the trading business again. Later on, Brushy had a ranch in Arkansas, near Oklahoma. He kept on riding bucking horses and doing anything he could do. He worked in the oil fields of Oklahoma. When oil was struck in east Texas, he went to Gladewater. He worked for the city of Gladewater as a plainclothesman. He aided Green, the Chief of Police. It was there that Brushy took part in breaking up a gang of bank robbers holed up in the Sabine River bottom.

*In the book, 'Billy the Kid: Killed in New Mexico----Died in Texas', by Jannay P. Valdez and Judge Bobby Hefner, the authors stated that Brushy married Ann White in Canton, Van Zandt County, Texas in 1908. Brushy apparently divorced Ann White and married Mollie Brown in 1912. But, as Brushy mentioned, he was ranching in Old Mexico from 1907 until 1914. When did he meet these women and where did he court them? These romances would have required considerable travel. But then Brushy was everywhere.*

*There is documented evidence that Oliver Pleasant Roberts married Anna Lee in 1909 and divorced her in 1910 after a court battle (See Appendices E, F, G, H, and I). There is also documented proof that he married Mollie Brown in 1912 (See Appendices J and K). All this happened in Van Zandt County Texas while Brushy was in Mexico. He must have had one fast horse or, again, he must have had the ability to be in more than one place at any given time. Actually, I'm somewhat surprised that Brushy didn't claim to have flown with the Wright Brothers.*

Mollie died in 1919. Brushy married Louticia Ballard in 1925. He lived with Louticia until her death in 1944 (See Appendix M). Then, he married Melinda Allison in November, 1944 (See Appendix N).

*About 1 o'clock P. M. on December 27, 1950, Brushy passed away in Hico, Texas. Who was this man? What was his real name? Was it William Henry Roberts, Oliver L. 'Brushy Bill' Roberts, or Oliver P. Roberts? He was going by Oliver L. in 1944 when he married Melinda Allison and when he died in 1950 (See Appendix O).*

*Was he born in 1859, 1868, or 1879? Brushy's original headstone had his birth date as 1868, but the current headstone has his birth date as 1859. It seems that originally someone miscalculated when Billy the Kid was actually born. Was Brushy really Billy the Kid? I believe the answer is rather obvious. As you read further, you will see Brushy was in fact Oliver Pleasant Roberts born August 26, 1879.*

# CHAPTER 7
## BRUSHY'S STORY ENDS
## HIS FINAL CHAPTER

Oliver Pleasant Roberts was born on August 26, 1879 in Bates, Sebastian County, Arkansas. His parents were Henry Oliver Roberts and Sarah Elizabeth Ferguson. Oliver Pleasant's grandparents on his father's side (Henry Oliver's parents) were Joseph Roberts and Rachel Henson (See Appendix U). Official records document the marriage of Joseph Roberts and Rachel Henson on July 28, 1844 in Rusk County, Texas. *A Memorial and Biographical History of Hill County, Texas* was published in 1892. In it the children of Joseph and Rachel were named as follows:

- Virgil A., in Erath Co., Texas, a prominent farmer;
- Amanda, the wife of the subject of this sketch (A. F. Branch);
- Samantha E., wife of E. Brown, married second time to Moses
- Ledwell, now a farmer in Erath;
- Henry O., a resident of Hopkins Co., Texas; and
- Andrew B., a prominent farmer of Denton Co., Texas."

Little is known of this Joseph Roberts beyond the fact he was born in Virginia and died in 1858. His death probably occurred in Rusk County Texas since he was involved in land transactions there on February 21, 1851 and August 31, 1858. Henry Oliver was born May, 1852 in Texas (according to the 1900 Hopkins Co., TX Census). Thus it is reasonable to assume that Henry Oliver's place of birth was in Rusk County Texas.

While Joseph Roberts' past is somewhat of a mystery, that of his wife Rachel Henson is not. Rachel was born September 11th, 1828 in either Rabun County or Gilmer County Georgia. Her parents were James B.

Henson and Elizabeth Ann Talley. James B. Henson was born August 25, 1802 probably in Pendleton District South Carolina. He died August 15, 1846 in Camargo, Mexico where he was on a campaign with Company G of the 2nd TX Mounted Volunteers. Elizabeth Ann Talley was born October 14, 1804 in Cherokee Nation-East (North Carolina). She died February 21, 1863 in Panola County Texas. Elizabeth Ann was a Cherokee Indian as is made clear in the following document in the 1999 Edition of *Cherokee Proud* as submitted by Tony McClure PH.D:

> **Cherokee Agency East Dec. 1st. 1835**
> **Lieut Van Horne**
> **US Disbursing Agent**
> **Sir**
> **I have just received a communication dated Nov.1835 from the (.....................)
> enclosing a copy of a communication from yourself to that department in relation to
> James B. Henson. His wife was represented to me to be of Cherokee blood but
> resided for many years among the whites and returned with Henson a white man into
> the Cherokee Country after the extension of the laws of Georgia. After he came into
> the county he was a candidate for the Legislature and was defeated on the score of his
> having an Indian blooded woman for a wife. This fact I was well satisfied of from my
> own knowledge but having doubts of his being really of Indian blood. I inquired of
> several persons of credibility who gave statement which removed my doubts and the
> family was consequently enrolled under the provision of the Treaty of May 6, 1828 as
> members of the Tribe. I had intended to have answered you fully by my
> communication of the 17 April last but suppose the name of James B. Henson was
> inadvertently overlooked.**
> **Very Respectfully Your Most Obt Servt**
> **Ben F. Currey**

Rachel Henson's brother, Henry Henson, the first born of James B. Henson and Elizabeth Ann Talley, deserves special mention for two reasons. First, he died in Van Zandt County Texas as did Henry O. Roberts. Second, he wrote the following fascinating life narrative that details the Henson family's early movements:

This bio is from the *Family Puzzler #1447*, 7/13/1996, p 5-7

**DR. H. HENSON REMEMBERS WHEN THE STARS FELL AND OTHER EVENTS OF EARLY DAYS:**

"I was born in Rabun County, Ga. May 21, 1823, which would make me between 85 and 86 years old. My father moved to Gilmore [Gilmer] County, Ga. where we lived until the spring of 1834"

"On the night of Nov 13, 1833, I saw the comets fall from the heavens by hundreds of thousands. The whole canopy of heaven was in a general commotion from midnight until daylight. I was not excited at the strange movements of the stars, as I supposed they did that every morning."

"Some movers, camped near our house, awoke and called out to my father that the world was coming to an end. I then got a little excited over it, and stated to my father that if that was anything to get excited over, I could have notified them two or three hours before. That was about 4:30 o'clock. I was 10 years old at the time of the falling of the stars. "

"In the spring of 1834 my father emigrated to Arkansas territory and afterwards to [the] Cherokee nation, where we remained one year. Later we lived in Benton County, Ark. where we ground all our meal, our family, seven in number, used on a steel mill ..."

"My father and family emigrated from Arkansas to Texas in 1841, stopping one year in Fannin County, and then moving to Rusk County, Tex. where we lived 7 years ..."

"I have lived under the administration of 22 presidents of the United States and two presidents of the republic of Texas, vs. Sam Houston and Anson Jones. The first vote I ever cast was for Anson Jones. The second one was the annexation of the republic of Texas to the United States in 1845 and I have never regretted casting that vote yet ..."

In the 1850 Texas census, there are a handful of Roberts born in Virginia as was Joseph Roberts. All are in the same general area; in counties bordering on or near to Rusk County Texas. In this small group is a Pleasant Roberts born about 1824, living in Red River County Texas in the household of Joseph J. Smith who married a Mrs. Mary K. Rider June 17, 1847 in Red River County Texas. Could this Pleasant Roberts be a brother of Joseph Roberts, father of Henry O. Roberts, father of Oliver Pleasant Roberts? In other words could this Pleasant Roberts be Oliver Pleasant's great uncle, and the source of Oliver's middle name? Red River County Texas marriage records indicate that Pleasant Roberts married Charlotte Williams on December 6th, 1850 in Red River County. However, census data strongly suggests that he in fact married Charlotte Perry, daughter of a Samuel and Sarah Perry on or about the same date.

In the book, *Alias Billy the Kid*, written by C. L. Sonnichsen and William V. Morrison, Brushy stated that his father was J. H. Roberts and that Sarah Elizabeth Ferguson was J. H. Roberts' second wife. Records clearly show that Sarah Elizabeth Ferguson was Henry Oliver Roberts' second wife, and that they were in fact the parents of Oliver P. Roberts, alias Brushy Bill. Morrison, the attorney who 'discovered' Brushy Bill, should have known who Brushy claimed as his father was and who his father married. It's clearly obvious that somebody erred. Was it Brushy, Morrison or both? Some later books about Brushy state that J. H. Roberts' second wife's name was unknown. In others it isn't mentioned at all. If Morrison accurately reported Brushy's story as Brushy told it, then Brushy got it wrong. Did later authors purposely gloss over these errors? They seem to have made a conscious effort to avoid this part of Brushy's story. Why?

In the family trees that appear in most books that support the Brushy Bill theory, Henry Oliver Roberts' father is shown to have been a Benjamin Roberts. No real proof has ever been offered to support that claim. As I have already discussed in some detail, Joseph Roberts was Henry Oliver's father. It has also been said that Henry O. was born in 1837 in Texas. Henry O. himself tells us four times in the censuses when he was born. The ages he gave, on three of the four censuses, reflect birth years between 1850 and 1853. On the other one, the 1900 census, he stated he was born May 1852. That agrees with the 1852 inscribed on his tombstone in Hillcrest Cemetery, Van Zandt Co., TX.

In the *Dallas Morning News*, an article written about Brushy Bill Roberts, dated September 18, 1950, the following was written,

**Bill is part Cherokee Indian, he vows. His mother was half Cherokee and his father was one-quarter Cherokee.**

It seems to be awful coincidental that both Brushy and Oliver Pleasant's fathers were one-quarter Cherokee. They did have different fathers and grandfathers, or didn't they? No, they had different fathers and their fathers were brothers. So, they had the same grandfather, Benjamin Roberts. No, that's not right; Oliver Pleasant's grandfather was Joseph Roberts. Now, I am really confused. Maybe their grandmothers on their fathers' side were the same. Oh, that's right; they were supposed to have the same grandmother, I think. One thing that we can say for sure is that Oliver Pleasant's mother was Brushy's stepmother, or at least they had the same name. No, we can't say that either. They had the same mother because they are one and the same person.

Henry Oliver was married first to Caroline Dunn around 1871. Caroline was born in Prairie, Franklin County, Arkansas in October 1850 and died in 1874. Henry O. and Caroline had two children, Samantha Belle, born Oct 1872, and Martha Vada, born September 3, 1873. Caroline was the daughter of Francis Dunn and either his wife Elizabeth Weaver Bolinger or his next wife Eve Telitha Counts. Elizabeth Weaver Bolinger died September 18, 1850 and is buried back in her birth place of Claiborne, County Tennessee.

Genealogy records reveal two conflicting dates for Francis Dunn's subsequent marriage to Eve Telitha Counts. One records their marriage as occurring on August 14, 1850, the other on December 14, 1850, both in Franklin County, Arkansas. To further complicate matters, when the census agent visited the household of Francis Dunn on November 26, 1850, Eve was present listed as a Dunn and Caroline was listed as one month old. Thus we have two possible scenarios. One, Francis Dunn and Elizabeth Weaver Bolinger divorced permitting the August 14, 1850 marriage to Eve Telitha Counts, which by virtue of Caroline's age, would suggest that Eve and Francis may have jumped the gun; a technicality that may have inspired the divorce. The other scenario is less messy but assumes slight errors as to this marriage date, Elizabeth's death date and/or Caroline's age. If Elizabeth died a month later than was recorded or if Caroline was a month older than recorded, then it is very likely that Elizabeth died giving birth to Caroline. Shortly thereafter, Francis married Eve Telitha who, by the way, was Elizabeth Weaver Bolinger's sister-in-law. Eve Telitha Counts was the widow of Samuel Bolinger, Elizabeth's brother. Complicated? Yes, but it gets worse.

Eve Telitha Counts and Samuel Bolinger were the parents of Martha Bolinger who married John W. Ferguson, who in turn were the parents of Sarah Elizabeth Ferguson, second wife of Henry O. Roberts. Martha is in the Francis Dunn 1850 household along with her Bolinger siblings, their mother Eve Telitha and Caroline Dunn. In this one household we have Henry O.'s first wife Caroline Dunn along with her step sister, Martha Bolinger, who will eventually become Henry O.'s mother-in-law. Francis Dunn was born in 1795 in Powell River Valley, Sullivan County, Tennessee. He served in the 2nd Corp of the East Tennessee Militia in the War of 1812. He died in December 1879 in Greenwood, Sebastian County, Arkansas and is buried there in the Mount Harmony Cemetery.

In the book, *The Return of the Outlaw Billy the Kid*, by W. C. Jameson, Mr. Jameson wrote that there were entries in a family bible that indicated that Catherine Bonney was a half sister to Caroline. However, there was no such family bible mentioned by Brushy in the book, 'Alias Billy the Kid', by Sonnichsen and Morrison. Was this bible only discovered after Brushy was dead and buried? Where is this bible now? Whose bible was it? What were the specific names and relationships in the bible that led the reader to conclude that Catherine Bonney was a half sister to Caroline Dunn?

Caroline Dunn did have a whole host of siblings, step, half, and possibly full. The split between half and full depends on whether her mother was Elizabeth Weaver Bolinger or Eve Telitha Counts (Bolinger) as discussed earlier. Eve Telitha Counts, widow of Samuel Bolinger (Elizabeth Weaver Bolinger's brother) provided Caroline with five step siblings when Eve married Caroline's father, Francis Dunn. Caroline had at least three known half siblings by an early marriage of Francis' to a woman generally believed to have been a Mary Lynch. After this marriage, Francis married Elizabeth Weaver Bolinger, a union that provided Caroline ten more siblings, half or full depending on the answer to the puzzle surrounding Caroline's mother. One of these siblings, a daughter by Elizabeth Weaver Bolinger, was named Catherine Dunn. She, however, married Samuel McFerran April 3, 1853 and then John Devore Keller August 19, 1866. Eleven of Caroline's eighteen siblings cited here (full or otherwise) were females. However, none was a Bonney; none married a Bonney; nor is anything to suggest that any of them even knew a Bonney.

It has also been written that Brushy's mother was Caroline's sister, Mary Adeline Dunn. Caroline did have a sister (or half sister) named Mary and a step-sister named Mary Bolinger, both age 13 and both living in same household as Caroline in 1850; that being the household of her father Francis Dunn and his wife or soon to be wife, Eve Telitha Counts (widow of Samuel Bolinger). There is no evidence that either was a Mary Adeline, which is debatable, but neither married a Roberts and fathered Brushy. More important the Franklin County Arkansas marriage records document one marrying Joseph Lane on June 19, 1853. The other is found in the 1860 census as Mary Bruton along with her two Bruton children in the household of Francis Dunn and Eve Telitha Counts. There is considerable irony though in his claim. Mary Bolinger, Caroline's step-sister, had a twin sister named Martha. This Martha Bolinger married John W. Ferguson on October 5, 1851. On February 24, 1856, they became the parents of Sarah Elizabeth who would marry Henry Oliver Roberts. Thus, there is no doubt that Sarah Elizabeth Ferguson was the mother of Oliver P. Roberts, alias Brushy Bill.

On June 1, 1880 the census taker visited the household of Henry and Elizabeth Roberts in Bates, Sebastian County Arkansas. The family names and ages, were as follows; Henry, 30, Elizabeth, 24, Samantha, 8, Martha, 6, Berry, 3, and Mary C., 2, and Oliver, 1. It's pretty clear that Brushy was leaving the starting gate a couple of decades or so later than he remembered.

It should be noted that Fort Smith is the county seat of Sebastian County. It's also where Isaac C. Parker, the "Hanging Judge", held court. This is the same judge for whom Brushy Bill claimed to have worked. Brushy was in the right neighborhood, but Judge Parker died November 17, 1896 when Brushy was 18 years old.

On June 5, 1900 Oliver Pleasant was recorded in the census still living with his family in Justice Precinct 7, Hopkins County, Texas. The family as recorded that day was as follows: Henry O. Roberts, born May 1852; his wife of 24 years, Sarah, born Feb 1856; and three sons; Oliver P., born Aug

1879; Thomas U., born Oct 1885; and Irvan, born Feb 1895. At least three other children, not listed here, were born to Henry O. and Sarah Elizabeth during the period between the 1880 and 1900 censuses. One child was John W. who is found in the cemetery records of Mount Harmony Cemetery, Greenwood, Sebastian County Arkansas. He died September 11, 1882 at the age of 1 year, 2 months and 24 days. His parents are listed as H. O. and S. E. Roberts. The other two children are Lonnie V. and Nora who are found in the cemetery records of Miller Grove Cemetery, Hopkins County Texas. Lonnie V. was born June 6$^{th}$, 1884 and died September 30$^{th}$, 1887; Nora, born April 29$^{th}$, 1892 and died May 6$^{th}$, 1893. Their parents are recorded as H. O. and S. E. Roberts.

In the book, *Billy the Kid: Killed in New Mexico—Died in Texas*, written by Dr. Jannay P. Valdez and Judge Bobby E. Hefner, the authors stated that Brushy Bill married an Ann White in Canton, Van Zandt County, Texas, in 1908 and was divorced (reason and date unknown). This was never mentioned by the authors in the book titled, *Alias Billy the Kid*, by C. L. Sonnichsen and William V. Morrison who recorded Brushy's story firsthand. Was this omission an oversight on their part or was it just something that Brushy thought would best be left unsaid?

On July 11, 1909, Oliver P. married Anna Lee in Van Zandt County, Texas (See Appendix E). In the 1910 census, Oliver P. Roberts is shown living with Anna in Van Zandt County, Texas. His age is listed as 30 and Anna's age as 22. Oliver and Anna divorced on November 10, 1910. Oliver filed for a divorce in September, 1910 due to incompatibility between himself and Anna (See Appendix F).

Is it just a coincidence that both Brushy Bill and Oliver P. married a woman named Ann and that both of their marriages ended shortly thereafter in divorce?

On August 21, 1912, Oliver Pleasant Roberts married Mollie Brown in Canton, Van Zandt County, Texas (See Appendix J). On a Draft Registration Card, dated September 12, 1918, Oliver is shown living with Mollie in Arkinda, Little River County Arkansas (See Appendix L). In the 1920 census, Oliver is shown as a widower and boarding with the James C. Murff family on Wills Point and Jackson Road in Precinct 1, District 122, Van Zandt County, Texas. His age is shown as 41. It is clear his wife, Mollie, died between the time he registered for the draft on September 12, 1918 and January 9$^{th}$, 1920 when he declared his widower status to the census taker.

In the book, *Alias Billy the Kid*, by Sonnichsen and Morrison, the authors state that Brushy Bill married Molly Brown of Coleman, Texas in 1912 and that she died in 1919. Another coincidence; Brushy and Oliver both married Mollie Browns in 1912 and then both Mollie Browns died around 1919. What are the odds? These odds get even longer when you consider that both Brushy and Oliver had previously had short marriages to women named Ann that ended in divorce.

On April 17, in the 1930 census, Oliver is shown living with his wife, Lutisha, in Precinct 1, District 6, Van Zandt County, Texas. His age is listed as 52 and his wife's age as 57 and that she was born in Missouri.

In the book, *Alias Billy the Kid*, by Sonnichsen and Morrison, the authors state that Brushy Bill married Louticia Ballard in 1925 and lived with her until her death. On her death certificate, it stated that she was born in Stoddard County, Missouri on July 13, 1875 and died in Van Zandt County, Texas on June 22, 1944 (See Appendix M). Also on her death certificate, her name was spelled 'Luticia'. Again, is it just a coincidence that Oliver P. and Brushy Bill married a Lutisha and a Louticia or Luticia in the 1920's? The accumulation of these coincidences is overwhelming to say the least.

Brushy Bill married Melinda E. Allison on January 14, 1945 in Hamilton County, Texas (See Appendix N). His name was listed as O. L. Roberts. Melinda died in 1952 in Temple, Texas.

I do not believe any of the so-called coincidences that I have cited were in fact really coincidences. They along with the other evidence prove beyond any reasonable doubt that Brushy Bill and Oliver Pleasant Roberts were one and the same person. Brushy Bill was Oliver Pleasant Roberts and he was born August 26, 1879 and died December 27, 1950 in Hico, Texas. Authors, that indorsed Brushy Bill's claims, accepted proof that was drawn up by Brushy Bill's own relatives, including bible entries. The documents that I used for Oliver Pleasant Roberts came from official records at government offices and genealogical societies. I think the proof of Brushy's real identity is overwhelming and will be accepted by all Billy the Kid enthusiasts.

In the same article mentioned earlier, in the *Dallas Morning News* dated September 18, 1950 about Brushy Bill, the following was stated:

**Brushy Bill--his real name, which he disdains, is Oliver L.--is the man who appeared on a New York radio show last January to backup the claim of an elderly Missourian, Frank Dalton, that he is Jesse James.**

**"Shore it's Jesse." he snaps. "I knowed him off and on for most of his life. First time I ever seen him I was about ten. He come to our house, wounded. Had a bullet hole in his shoulder you could see daylight through. I watched my mother wrap a rag 'round a stick, put something on it and swab out the hole. In New York, I seen the scars on Jesse. I'd never forget how he looked--six feet, 180 pounds, fair complected, sandy hair, bird-gander blue eyes, and full forehead."**

**'I was born in Buffalo Gap in Taylor County, the last hour of 1859. My**

granddad, Ben Roberts, was with Gen. Sam Houston in the Mexican War. He got that fancy cane hangin' there. My dad, J. H. Roberts--everybody called him Wild Henry--come from Kentucky in 1850. He was a scout with Kit Carson--him and Carson tried to warn Custer he couldn't lick them five tribes of Indians but he wouldn't listen. So they took out. And they was right."

"We come to this country when I was about seven. Dad taught me to ride horses. I could ride anything you could throw a rope on. Boylike, I got mad at him, left home when I was fifteen. Never saw him again. I headed for Indian Territory, Oklahoma now. Near a town called Briartown I met Belle Starr. I was walking and she was ridin'. She was wearin' two six-shooters, looked like a man. Her and Jesse James was sweethearts for a while. She was about thirty and mighty good lookin'."

Bill spent several months at Belle Starr's place, he says. He never took part in any holdups, but he did hold the horses out in the brush one time for the gang. Still a kid, he moved on, falling in with roving bands often. Once he became a member of a gang of horse thieves, unknowingly, but he scooted quick.

In fact, for many years he made a good, if precarious, living chasing down horse thieves. Part of the time he had a half-breed helper, named Indian Jim. He was wounded twenty-six times and lost thirty horses in scrapes with thieves, he says proudly. He saw many a horse thief at the end of a rope.

He wandered through Texas, Oklahoma, New Mexico, and Kansas when he was still a teen-age kid. But he could handle a six-gun, ride anything with four legs, and handle his fists, he says. When he was twenty-one he was guard for a stagecoach in the Dakota Black Hills. He weathered four holdup attempts. Dakota was too cold, so he headed back south. For seven years, he recalls, he ranched in Mexico.

Brushy's dad, J. H. Roberts was a scout with Kit Carson. That could have been. His dad and Kit Carson tried to warn General Custer "he couldn't beat those five Indian tribes." Well, let's see, Kit Carson died in 1868 and the Battle of Little Big Horn took place in 1876. And, there were six tribes, not five.

Jesse James went to Brushy's house when Brushy was 10 years old. Did Jesse go to Indianapolis, Indiana? I really doubt it.

Many people said that Brushy Bill looked young for his age. Well, it appears there was good reason for his youthful appearance. He wasn't as old as he claimed, and he certainly wasn't old enough to have been Billy the Kid.

In the same story in the *Dallas Morning News*, this was written:

Brushy Bill is Hico's best-known character. He says he's ninety. He looks twenty years younger. His gaze is piercing, his voice strong, and his hearing perfect.

And guess what? *The Dallas Morning News* got it right!

Subsequent books written after *Alias Billy the Kid* have changed some details and added a lot of information that seems to have been intended to make Brushy's life better fit that of Billy the Kid's. Remember it was Mr. Morrison who interviewed Brushy. Right or wrong, Mr. Morrison got the story from the horse's own mouth. I just find it hard to believe that this "new information", as cited by later authors, in support of Brushy's case, would not have been mentioned by Brushy himself, if it were true. The subsequent books that I will be referencing are, *Billy the Kid: Killed in New Mexico--Died in Texas* by Dr. Jannay P. Valdez and Judge Bobby E. Hefner, *The Return of the Outlaw Billy the Kid* by W. C. Jameson and Frederic Bean, and *Billy the Kid, Beyond the Grave* by W. C. Jameson. Following are some of these differences:

- Sonnichsen and Morrison stated Brushy's father was J. H. Roberts. Valdez and Hefner said that it was John Henry while Jameson said it was James Henry in both his books.

- Sonnichsen and Morrison Brushy referred to his aunt as Kathrine Ann Bonney. Valdez and Hefner referred to his aunt as Katherine Bonney McCarty. They also said that her husband was Michael McCarty and he died in the Civil War in 1865. Jameson referred to his aunt as Catherine Ann Bonney in his first book and Katherine Ann Bonney in his latest book.

- Sonnichsen and Morrison never mentioned Brushy's aunt's marriage to William Antrim on March 1, 1873. They said that Brushy was in Texas with his real family. Valdez and Hefner mentioned the marriage, but did not mention that Brushy was at the wedding. Jameson mentioned the wedding in his first book, but also failed to mention Brushy being there. Jameson failed to mention the marriage at all in his latest book.

- Sonnichsen and Morrison stated that Brushy's father married Sarah Ferguson of Tennessee. Valdez and Hefner said that his wife's name was unknown. Jameson stated her name was Sarah Ferguson in both of his books.

- Sonnichsen and Morrison said that Brushy's aunt first went to Trinidad, Colorado, then to Santa Fe, and then to Silver City, New Mexico. Valdez and Hefner said Brushy's aunt took him to her home in Indian Territory, then to Marion County, Indiana in 1866, and then to Wichita, Kansas in 1869. Still according to Valdez and Hefner, Brushy then went back to 'the buffalo gap', Texas in 1872 to see his former family, went on some cattle drives with his dad, and then returned to Wichita, Kansas. His new family then packed up and went to Colorado, then Santa Fe, and finally to Silver City, New Mexico (Remember, the movements of the real Henry McCarty and his family are well documented from Wichita, Kansas in 1871; to Santa Fe, New Mexico where in 1873 his mother married William Antrim; to Silver City New Mexico where his mother died in 1874). Jameson echoed essentially the same pattern of movements described by Sonnichsen and Morrison with this exception. Jameson wrote that Brushy left New Mexico in 1873 and went to Buffalo Gap, Texas and then finally to Carlton, Texas where he found his former family.

I could go on and on pointing out differences in the authors' stories, but I think you have seen enough to recognize the problems. You have to remember that there was only one Brushy and he told only one story. That story was told to Mr. Morrison. Subsequent authors seem to have gone far beyond Brushy's original story in a futile attempt to make Brushy's story match closer that of the real Billy the Kid. Why didn't these authors stick with Brushy's own story? Could it be that the facts just didn't support it? Give Brushy his due. He told a wonderful story; a real whopper; but, it was fiction.

I have other circumstantial evidence that will help sway any remaining doubters. Some of it was previously mentioned, but I feel it to be important enough to repeat. If you still believe Brushy Bill's claims, then you must continue reading. I am confident you will see the holes, false claims, and impossibilities in his story. Originally I, too, thought that Brushy Bill might have been Billy the Kid; but the more I tried to prove it, the more obvious it became that it just wasn't so.

- In the book, *The West of Billy the Kid*, by Frederick Nolan, he states that Billy the Kid was in Arizona from 1875-1877. In the book, *Alias Billy the Kid*, Brushy said that about the first of April, 1877, he and Mountain Bill went to Arizona to visit Bill's sister and that they worked a few months on the Gila Ranch. Before that, Brushy said that he was everywhere but Arizona.

- In the book, *Alias Billy the Kid*, Brushy said that he and Tom O'Keefe left Mesilla in the summer of 1877 for Loving's Bend near Phoenix, New Mexico. It is generally accepted as fact that Henry McCarty alias Kid Antrim killed Frank P. Cahill on August 17$^{th}$, 1877 and didn't arrive in Mesilla until some time after that. There is no mention in the book of Brushy killing Cahill, the event that caused Henry to flee Arizona.

- In the book, *Alias Billy the Kid*, Brushy stated that he was in Old Mexico from 1907 to 1914. But, in the book, *Billy the Kid: Killed in New Mexico—Died in Texas*, by Valdez and Hefner, the authors state that Brushy married Ann White in 1908 in Canton, Texas and was divorced shortly thereafter; and then married Mollie Brown in Canton, Texas in 1912. How could Brushy be in Old Mexico when he was marrying, divorcing, and remarrying in Canton, Texas? Canton is in Van Zandt County Texas.

- Brushy made no mention of his early life in Indianapolis. Henry McCarty spent at least 5 years there. Granted he would have been very young at the time, but he should have remembered something about it. Even if he didn't, somebody would have surely told him of it.

- Henry's time spent in Wichita, Kansas had to be a turning point in his life. He spent almost two years there. He was 10 to 12 years old, so he had to have remembered something. These were exciting times in Wichita. It was at the height of the big cattle drives from Texas through Wichita to the markets further north. There were a lot of wild cowboys and action during that period, a lot of drinking, gambling, and gun fights. Life there would have been filled with memorable events. Brushy, however, doesn't even mention living in Wichita.

- Joseph McCarty (Antrim) was never mentioned by Brushy. Henry McCarty and Joseph grew up together, and they are believed by most historians to have been brothers. Even if they weren't brothers, they would have been very close. They spent at least a decade of their early childhood under the same roof; they traveled about the country together; they attended Catherine McCarty's wedding together; and before going their separate ways, they undoubtedly attended Catherine's funeral together. Henry McCarty would have thought Joseph worthy of mention. Brushy did not.

- Brushy never mentioned William Antrim even though he would have played a big part in his life; that is of course, if Brushy was Henry McCarty. William H. Antrim married Mrs. Catherine McCarty in 1873 Santa Fe New Mexico. Brushy claims that this Catherine was his half aunt. Well, the marriage record lists Henry McCarty and Joseph McCarty as witnesses to the marriage and clearly identifies both as sons of Mrs. Catherine McCarty. Could Bushy really forget his step-father's name? Joseph lived the rest of his life as an Antrim. Henry used it as an alias.

- Brushy never mentioned his early life in Silver City. Henry McCarty's life there has been well chronicled and documented. Wouldn't Brushy have remembered his experiences in school, his close friends, and the events there, that would forever change his life? Henry McCarty would have thought them important. But then Brushy said he was in Texas with his real family at this time. So Brushy, by his own admission, simply didn't have the opportunity to experience Henry McCarty's early years in Silver City.

- Brushy makes very little mention of his Aunt Catherine's sickness and death. His Aunt Catherine would have been one of the most important people in his life. She was supposed to have saved him from a ruthless father and she was the only mother that he had really ever known. By all accounts, she was one of, if not, the most important person in Henry McCarty's early life. That of course, as we have noted earlier, was because she was Henry McCarty's mother.

- Brushy said little about his life and experiences in Arizona. Henry McCarty would have had far more to say about Arizona and he would have recognized the importance of saying it – if he wanted to be believed. Obviously, Brushy wanted to be believed. So why didn't he elaborate more? Could it be he was never in Arizona?

- Brushy seldom mentioned his girlfriends or his love life, and when he did, it was obvious that he was lying. William H. Bonney, had a lot of girlfriends during his days in New Mexico. In fact, one in particular, in the Pete Maxwell household, was important enough to die for. Wouldn't Brushy find her worthy of mention? William H. Bonney, certainly would have, but then he died in the Maxwell house in 1881.

We can forgive Brushy for all these errors and inconsistencies. He had a very good excuse for not being able to recall this part of his life in any detail. His excuse was quite simple and even more obvious - he hadn't been born when most of these events occurred, and he was only two years old when William H. Bonney was shot by Pat Garrett. Brushy was Oliver Pleasant Roberts. Again, Brushy himself, told us his date of birth when he registered for the WWI draft on September 12, 1918. He signed it "Oliver Pleasant Roberts".

I believe you get the idea. Brushy seems to have talked only about those aspects Billy the Kid's life with which he was familiar and that would give credence to his own claim. Unfortunately, for Brushy, there was a lot about Billy's life that he did not know. Much of this lack of knowledge is quite understandable. It wasn't available to Brushy because it hadn't been published yet. Brushy in his story tried to convey macho traits of toughness, bravery, and superiority that he believed fit the image of Billy the Kid – at least that of the "Kid" of whom he had read and of whom he had heard stories.

Those who actually knew Billy, in his William H. Bonney days, tell a quite different story. Their accounts reveal a more human side, a polite young man who carried groceries for old ladies, who enjoyed holding babies, who loved the senoritas, and who was loved by the senoritas. There was no rejoicing in Fort Sumner in the wake of Billy's death. The citizens did not hail Pat Garrett as a hero. Their reaction was quite the opposite – sympathy and grief for Billy; anger and even hatred for Garrett. This reaction was not borne of Billy's macho tough guy reputation, but of his more endearing qualities long remembered by those who knew him. Billy had a human side, a romantic and caring personality, and a desire to go straight and live a good life. He made it very clear in his dealings with Governor Lew Wallace that he wanted to get out of the outlaw business.

I suspect that the authors of the original book, *Alias Billy the Kid'* had their own doubts about Brushy Bill's claims. They had to have recognized that a lot of Brushy's information was unrealistic and contradictory. Why didn't they follow-up on the problem areas? Either the right questions weren't asked or they were asked, and not satisfactorily answered. Among the questions that I feel should have been asked of Brushy Bill are the following:

- What happened to your real father, step-mother, and half brother? Why didn't you search for them when you returned to Texas?

- Did your family know that you were Billy the Kid?

- Where was your real mother buried? How did she die?

- Can you tell me more about Billy Barlow, your friend that Pat Garrett killed? Where did you meet him and when? Did he say anything about his family, his background, or where he had lived?

- Since you were not killed by Pat Garrett, why did so many of your friends say you were? If your friends didn't know it was you, how could they have been so easily fooled? If no one liked Garrett, why didn't someone tell the truth about what really happened? Some had decades in which to set the record straight. Why didn't they? The Mexican women that doctored your wounds that night, as well As Celsa and Frank Lobato 'knew' that you didn't die. Why did they remain silent and allow Pat Garrett to become a hero and collect the reward money?

- Why didn't anyone ever mention the gun battle between you and Garrett's posse after Billy Barlow was killed? Who did Garrett and his posse think they were shooting at? Did Garrett know it was William Bonney? If Garrett had killed or captured you when you were trying to get away, how would he have explained his killing of Billy Barlow? It would have been murder!

- What do you think happened to A. J. Fountain and his son? Who would have wanted them dead? Were you involved?

-Who do you really think killed Pat Garrett? Did you have anything to do with it?

- You said that you did not want to leave New Mexico until after John Chisum, Barney Mason, and Pat Garrett were dead? Did you ever try to find Garrett since you were so intent on seeing him dead?

- Why didn't you go by your real name William Henry Roberts after you returned to Texas since no one knew that you were William Bonney. You knew that all of your family, including your kin in east Texas and in Hamilton County would remember your real name anyway. How did you explain your name change to them?

- Your cousin, Oliver P. Roberts was almost 20 years younger than you. How were you able to fool his mother into thinking that you were her long lost son? Oliver's brother-in-law knew better, so, why didn't his mother know better? How were you able to fool Oliver's own brothers and sisters?

If you had fooled everyone into believing you were Ollie P. Roberts, why did you then change it to Ollie L. Roberts?

Why Mr. Morrison didn't ask more questions and more pertinent questions, we will never know. If Brushy had been the real Billy the Kid, he could have cleared up a lot of the mystery that surrounds him. But, as we know, he would have identified Brushy as a fake to the rest of the world.

I hope as you read this chapter that you kept in mind that the book, *Alias Billy the Kid* was written by Sonnichsen and Morrison. Sonnichsen was a professor at the University of Texas at El Paso. He was a historian of the old Southwest and he won many awards for his writings. Mr. Morrison was the lawyer who discovered Brushy Bill. He interviewed him, recorded their conversations, read his notebooks and took notes. Morrison took Brushy to New Mexico to see Governor Mabry in hopes of getting the pardon that had been originally promised to Billy the Kid. While in New Mexico, they toured Billy's old stomping grounds.

There is one more piece of evidence that I have withheld until now - just in case you haven't made up your mind yet. According to Brushy's niece, Mrs. Geneva Pittmon, Brushy Bill was born on August 26, 1879 (See Appendix T). She also said she had the family Bible records to prove it. According to her family Bible records, Oliver Pleasant (Brushy) was her father's, Tom Robert's, brother. Official records substantiate her claims that Tom Roberts was the brother of Oliver Pleasant Roberts and that she was the daughter of Tom Roberts.

I have found no public records for Oliver Pleasant Roberts after the 1930 census. On the other hand, I have found no public records for Oliver L. Roberts dated before 1944. The records I did find on Oliver L. were his marriage license when he married Melinda and his death certificate.

The last piece of important information that I want to share is the evidence that Brushy might have used the book, *The Saga of Billy the Kid,* written by Walter Noble Burns in 1926, as a guide for his story. Following are some of the questionable coincidences.

-    Both Brushy and Mr. Burns referred to the Five Day Battle as he 'Three-Day Battle'.

-    Both Brushy and Mr. Burns referred to 'Kip' McKinney as 'Tip' McKinney.

-    Both Brushy and Mr. Burns said that Brushy/Bonney and Waite crawled over the wall and approached Sheriff Brady's body when it was really Bonney and Jim French.

-    Both Brushy and Mr. Burns said that Morton and Baker tried to escape and Brushy/Bonney killed them both.

-    Both Brushy and Mr. Burns said that Ollinger went across the street from the Lincoln courthouse to eat at noon when it was actually 5 o'clock in the evening.

What are the odds of both of Brushy and Mr. Burns making the exact same mistakes? I would say that it would be almost impossible.

It is true that Brushy didn't follow Mr. Burns book all the time because Brushy's own story could not be told if he followed the book. For instance, Brushy said that he went to Oklahoma after his Aunt Catherine's death, where Mr. Burns said that Henry McCarty went to Arizona after his mother, Catherine, died. Brushy inserted his own statements in order that his story would seem believable.

Well, if you still think Brushy Bill was Billy the Kid, then I just have to say that you are entitled to your opinion and you can't be persuaded otherwise. I've done my best here to set the record straight. I can say, without any reservations, that Brushy Bill was not Billy the Kid. Brushy Bill should be remembered for who he really was, Oliver Pleasant Roberts, a storyteller.

# CHAPTER 8
## BILLY THE KID
## FINDING HIS ORIGIN

There have been many, many books, magazine articles, and newspaper articles written about Billy the Kid, who he was, where he was born, and who his parents were. Fact invariably becomes confused with fiction. Was Billy born in New York, Ireland, Indiana, Illinois, or none of the above? Was Billy born in September, 1859, November, 1859, or neither? Was Catherine McCarty his real mother or his aunt or adoptive mother? Was her maiden name Bonney, McCarty, or something else? Was Catherine born in Ireland, New York, Indiana, Illinois, Ohio, or somewhere else? Was Catherine married to William Bonney, Michael McCarty, or only to William Antrim? Was Joseph, Billy's brother, a cousin, or no kin at all? Was Joseph older or younger than Billy? Was Joseph born in New York, Indiana, or neither?

These questions remain largely unanswered, but many of the more recent historians and authors have reached a consensus on some of them, right or wrong. As to some questions, official records and documents that have yet to be unearthed will be the final arbitrator of right and wrong. As to others, proof with complete certainty may never be found. Where proof is lacking, we depend on circumstantial evidence as a basis on which to formulate plausible theories. It will be the responsibility of historians and authors to form such theories carefully and clearly identify them as such.

The first nonfiction book written about Billy the Kid, *The Authentic Life of Billy the Kid*, was in fact mostly fiction. It was ghost written by Ash Upson for Pat Garrett. While some of the events in the book may have actually happened, the details surrounding them are more often than not, pure fiction. Far too many later authors relied on this book for their 'facts'. They have repeated them so many times in subsequent books that it has become almost impossible to separate fact from fiction. Historians and authors tend to accept information as fact when provided by the actual players. In the case of Upson and Garrett, it was a huge mistake.

Some of the first bogus statements made by Ash Upson relate to Billy's birth and early childhood. The following statements were made in the opening of the book:

**William H. Bonney, hero of this history was born in the city of New York, November 23, 1859. But little is known of his father, as he died when Billy was very young, and he had little recollection of him. In 1862, the family, consisting of the father, mother, and two boys, of whom Billy was the eldest, emigrated to Coffeyville, Kansas. Soon after settling there the father died, and the mother with her two boys removed to Colorado, where she married a man named Antrim, who is said to be now living at, or near, Georgetown, in Grant County, New Mexico, and is the only survivor of the family of four, who removed to Santa Fe, New Mexico, shortly after their marriage.**

There is no proof for these statements, nor is their any circumstantial evidence that suggests even a basis for them. The name, 'William H. Bonney', is universally conceded to be an alias that Billy used, with his real name being Henry McCarty. Why he chose this alias is unknown. If Billy in fact ever claimed 'New York' as his birthplace, he probably did so to help hide his real identity. If he was using an alias, it is unlikely he would reveal his birthplace. 'November 23' was Ash Upson's month and day of birth. What are the odds that Ash and Billy would share the same date of birth? Also, Upson stated that William Antrim was the sole survivor of the family of four. Joe (McCarty) Antrim was still living.

Billy and his family moved to 'Coffeyville, Kansas' in 1862? Prior to 1869, there was nothing on the site that would become Coffeyville. It was not until 1869 that Colonel James A. Coffey arrived from Humboldt, Kansas and founded an Indian trading post on the site. The town first incorporated in 1872, and re-incorporated in March of 1873. If Billy and his family were there in 1862, they would have been very lonely. 'Antrim' and Henry's 'mother' met in Indiana and married in 'Santa Fe, New Mexico', not in Colorado. Their marriage documents found in Santa Fe prove this beyond any doubt.

Ash Upson also stated:

**These facts are all that can be gleaned of Billy's early childhood, which, up to this time, would be of no interest to the reader.**

The writers were obviously hoping that Billy's childhood would be of no interest to the readers, since they knew nothing of it.

In the book, *History of "Billy the Kid"* by Charles A. Siringo, Mr. Siringo stated:

> **In the slum district of the great city of New York, on the 23rd day of November, 1859, a blue-eyed baby boy was born to William H. Bonney and his good looking wife, Kathleen. Being their first child, he was naturally the joy of their hearts. Later, another baby boy followed. In 1862, William H. Bonney shook the dust of New York City from his shoes and immigrated to Coffeyville, Kansas, on the northern border of the Indian Territory, with his family. Soon after.................**

The rest are direct quotations from Pat Garrett's book. The only thing new of seeming importance added by Mr. Siringo is a new father's name. But is it true? Where's the proof? He also adds that this first child:

> **was naturally the joy of their hearts.**

Now how did he know that? From where did he get this intimate little detail? Where is the proof, the documentation, or even the rationale for any of Mr. Siringo's declarations concerning this event? Note as well that Mr. Siringo's William H. Bonney:

> **shook the dust of New York City from his shoes and immigrated to Coffeyville, Kansas in 1862.**

We have already clearly established that Coffeyville, Kansas did not exist in 1862.

In the book, *The Saga of Billy the Kid*, by Walter Noble Burns, Mr. Burns wrote:

> **Throughout his life of lurid adventure, Billy the Kid's name was lost in his pseudonym. His name really doesn't matter much; by any other, he would have shot as straight; but it happened to be William H. Bonney, and he was born in New York City, November 23, 1859. William H. and Kathleen Bonney, his parents, both of unknown antecedents, immigrated in 1862 to Coffeyville, Kansas, taking with them three-year-old Billy and a baby brother named Edward.**

Sound familiar? The only change here was to rename Joseph to Edward. Mr. Noble was also wrong about Billy's name not being important. He not only relied on Ash Upson for many of his facts, but he also adopted Ash's rationale that facts unknown to the author will not be important to the readers. It is indeed odd though, that after offering their own so-called facts as to Billy's origins, these authors then minimized their importance by declaring them of no interest to the reader. Maybe they felt the need to provide such a disclaimer since they knew their facts were not facts at all?

In the book, *Alias Billy the Kid, The Man behind the Legend* by Donald Cline, Mr. Cline writes:

**It has long been known, and proven, that William Bonney was born Henry McCarty and later known as Henry Antrim. Henry McCarty was born in the predominately Irish Fourth Ward section of east-side Manhattan on November 20, 1859. He first saw light of day in private furnishing at 70 Allen Street. Though he was not fortunate to have entered this world through a hospital like his older brother, Joe, they shared a common bond: they were both illegitimate.**

Mr. Cline states that the proof for Henry McCarty's birth is found in the Municipal Archives & Records Center, New York City. As to Henry's brother Joseph, Mr. Cline writes:

**According to Joe's death certificate, he died at 76 years of age, which by my calculations, makes the year of his birth 1854. Some have tried to incorrectly state that Joseph was younger than Henry but he was not. During the years 1852-1856 there was only one male child named McCarty born in the entire city of New York and that was Joseph M. McCarty. According to the birth records, he was born August 25, 1854, at the New York Hospital located at 525 East 68th Street. Catherine McCarty is listed as the mother. No listing is given for the father.**

Such specificity conveyed with such authority, one would have to believe that Mr. Cline has done his research. But has he? I seriously doubt it. Probably the most outrageous claim made here is that:

**During the years 1852-1856 there was only one male child named McCarty born in the entire city of New York and that was Joseph M. McCarty.**

If anybody believes that claim, I've got a bridge in nearby Brooklyn that I'll sell them cheap! A quick check of the censuses reveals that at least 77 McCarty males were born in New York City during that period. This is counting only the ones that the indexers spelled as McCarty. There were undoubtedly countless other McCarty male children in that era whose names were misspelled by the indexers and/or the census agents. The real number doesn't matter. The point is that to claim Joseph McCarty was the only male McCarty child born in New York City during that five year period, is simply ridiculous. I don't doubt that Mr. Cline has found a birth certificate for his Joseph M. McCarty. However, I seriously doubt if his Joseph M. McCarty is the right Joseph McCarty. How did he make the link? Where's the proof?

Speaking of proof, Mr. Cline's states that proof of Henry McCarty's birth:

**is found in the Municipal Archives & Records Center, New York City.**

Is he saying he found a record of Billy the Kid's birth and didn't copy it, transcribe it, or even note the file in which it was found?

Mr. Cline's Joseph:

**was born August 25, 1854, at the New York Hospital located at 525 East 68th Street.**

He cites Joseph's death certificate, which states he died in 1930 at 76 years of age, as proof that he was born in 1854. While he is right about the math, it is generally conceded by all that Joseph's age, as stated on his death certificate, was in error. Most historians and authors now believe that Joseph was younger than Henry alias Billy the Kid. At his mother's wedding Joseph's name was listed in the *Book of Marriages* as "Josie," an acceptable nickname for a youngster, but not a young man of 18 or 19. The Silver City newspaper reported that Joseph Antrim:

**was among the children who spoke at the Christmas Tree and New Year's Eve Festival held in the City Hall on Thursday evening, December 30, 1875.**

So here again he is portrayed more in the mold of a youngster than that of a young man. In the 1880 Census, Joseph was in Silverton, San Juan County Colorado where his age was recorded as 17. The census records abound with young men who claimed to be older than they were. But it would have been rare, if not unheard of, for a 26 year old man to have claimed he was 17. How did Mr. Cline know that both Joseph and Henry were illegitimate? How did he know that it was in a "private furnishing" that Henry first saw the light of day?

Later on in his book, Mr. Cline wrote:

**That Catherine McCarty remained in New York City until 1873 is verified by policeman Dwyer, twenty close companions and records of New York City.**

If Mr. Cline is correct about this Catherine remaining in New York City until 1873, then he has proved beyond any reasonable doubt that she is not Catherine McCarty, mother of Henry alias Billy the Kid. The evidence is irrefutable that Catherine McCarty lived in Wichita, Kansas in 1870 and 1871.

In W. E. Koop's book, *Billy the Kid, The trail of a Kansas Legend*, Mr. Koop provided a lot of proof that Catherine McCarty and William H. Antrim lived there in Wichita, Kansas in 1871 and 1872. Mr. Koop stated that Colonel Marsh Murdock wrote in the *Wichita Weekly Eagle* on August 11, 1881 the following:

**Billy the Kid, an account of whose tragic death we published two weeks since, formerly lived in Wichita, and many of the early settlers remember him as a street gamin in the days of longhorns.**

Mr. Koop goes on to write,

**The earliest known record of her Kansas transactions may be noted in various entries in Sedgwick county deed records which indicate that on September 12, 1870, Mrs. Catherine McCarty was given title to a vacant lot on Chisholm (now Market) street in the city of Wichita. Numerous other entries were found, too numerous in fact, for inclusion here, but all dealt with the real estate purchases of Catherine McCarty. Of further interest are the entries, which reveal that in February of 1871, William H. Antrim was given title to neighboring lots on Chisholm Street. All of these entries, indicating modestly extensive holdings in what was then the hub and center of the village's business district, give an entirely different view of the legendary picture of an impoverished widow barely able to make ends meet for the family of two growing boys.**

Mr. Koop stated that on March 15, 1871, the editor of the *Wichita Tribune* brought out his salutatory edition. And in giving free "puffs" to various local businesses he commented:

**The City Laundry is kept by Mrs. McCarty, to whom we recommend those who wish to have their linen made clean.**

Mr. Koop goes on to say that on March 25, 1871, Catherine McCarty presented herself at the nearby Augusta, Kansas to lay claim to some property that she had improved and homesteaded. To support her claim Antrim submitted a sworn statement as follows:

**LAND OFFICE, Augusta, Kansas, March 25, 1871.**
**In the matter of the application of Catharine McCarty of Sedgwick County, Kansas to purchase the northwest Quarter of Section No. 12 in Township No. 27 South, in Range No. 1 East, under the provisions of the Joint resolution of Congress approved April 10, 1869, for the disposal of the lands ceded by the Osage Indians under the Second Article of the Treaty of September 29, 1865.**
**Personally appeared the said Catharine McCarty and offered proof in support of her application, as follows, viz: William Antrim of lawful age being duly sworn, deposes and says: I have known Catharine McCarty for 6 years past: that she is a single woman over the age of twenty-one years, the head of a family consisting of two**

children, a citizen of the United States, and a bona fide settler upon the foregoing described land, which she seeks to purchase, having settled thereon about the 10 day of August, 1870; on or about the 10 day of August, 1870 he built a house upon said lands, 12 by 14 feet, 1 story high, board floor, 1 door and 2 windows. She moved into said house with her family and effects on or about the 4$^{th}$ day of March A. D. 1871, and has resided in said house and upon said land to the present time, and that she has made the following additional improvements on said land: She has about 7 acres enclosed and in cultivation. She has 640 rods hedge row about 7 ft. wide, She has posts and rails on ground for further fencing. She has a well 12 ft. deep. She has 57 fruit trees set and growing. She has an outdoor cellar 6x8 ft. covered with earth and timbers. I estimate the value of improvements at from $250 to $300 dollars.

Wm. H. Antrim

Sworn to and subscribed before me this 25$^{th}$ of March, A. D. 1871

W. A. Shannon, Receiver

Frederick Daily of lawful age being by me first duly sworn according to law deposes and says, I have known Catharine McCarty for the ten months last past and know of my own personal knowledge that the allegations herein contained are substantially correct and true.

Fredrick Daily

Sworn to and subscribed before me this 25$^{th}$ day of March, 1871

W. A. Shannon, Receiver

This application was stated in full because of its significant implications. William Antrim said,

I have known Catharine McCarty for six years past.

This means that they met sometimes around 1864 or 1865. Fredrick Daily said,

I have known Catharine McCarty for the ten months last past.

This means that she must have arrived in Wichita around May or June 1870. These important points can help historians and authors determine their movements and the timing of these movements before coming to Wichita.

In the book, *Billy the Kid, A Date with Destiny* by Carl W. Breihan, with Marion Ballert, Mr. Breihan wrote:

The generally accepted date and place of Billy's birth is November 23, 1859 in New York City although his "second best friend", George Coe, (George's cousin, Frank, being his first, according to Billy) gives it as November 29, 1859 in his autobiography, 'Frontier Fighter.' According to the record in the United States Census, it is November 23, 1859. His parents were William H. and Catherine Bonney, who came from New Orleans to New York about six months prior to the Kid's birth.

These statements sound just like Garrett and Upson except now the Bonneys were in New Orleans and Billy's birth date is November 29, 1859. I am not sure which census records that Mr. Breihan was looking through, because I have never found birth dates included until the 1900's. Never was the day of birth listed and only in the 1900 census was the month of birth ever listed.

In the book, *A Fitting Death for Billy the Kid*, by Ramon F. Adams, Mr. Adams stated,

**The Kid is supposed to have been born in New York City, November 23, 1859, but no records have ever been found to substantiate this date. It is based solely upon Ash Upson's questionable authority.**

Well, Mr. Adams can see through Upson's lack of credibility. No records have been found to support the claim that the Kid was born in New York, probably because he was not born there. Mr. Adams does not even speculate as to where and when Billy was born. That was in fact the responsible way to handle what otherwise would have been speculation without any evidentiary basis. If Ash Upson had exercised similar restraint, the Billy the Kid picture of today would be far less confusing.

In the book, *Goodbye Billy the Kid*, by Harold L. Edwards, Mr. Edwards stated:

**Although no documents have surfaced to prove the place and time of Henry McCarty's birth, most authorities on his life concur that he was born in New York City on November 23, 1859.**

The authorities to who he refers were clearly those who had depended on Ash Upson and Pat Garrett for their 'facts'. An authority is not one who just claims to know the facts, but one who can support those facts with proof. Claiming something to be true, does not make it true, no matter how many times it is repeated. Claims of fact must be supported with proof. If they can not be proven, then they are simply not facts.

In the book, *Billy the Kid, The Story – The Trial*, by Randy Russell, Mr. Russell stated:

**Born in New York City in 1859 as Henry McCarty, during his lifetime he was also known as Henry Antrim, Austin Antrim, William H. Antrim, William H. Bonney, "Kid" and finally as the infamous "Billy the Kid.**

Mr. Russell played it safe and used Ash Upson's fictitious date like most of the other authors. I do not know where he got the alias, Austin Antrim, but I will not argue with him. It would have been nice though if he had he told us.

Frederick Nolan's book, *The West of Billy the Kid*, seems to be the most accurate account of Billy the Kid's life that I have ever read. Mr. Nolan does not mix fact with fiction. He does present interesting theories, but he makes it very clear that they are just theories, nothing more. I think he is very close to discovering the birth site of Henry McCarty and the truth about his and Joseph's origins. If there was ever an expert on Billy the Kid, Mr. Nolan is the person. He approached writing his book with an open mind and the determination to find and print the truth.

We know that Billy the Kid was not John Miller born in Texas or Oklahoma, nor was he William Henry Roberts born in Buffalo Gap, Texas. Then where and when was he born? The simple answer is "we don't know." He could have been born anywhere between about 1855 and 1863. As we have seen the answers offered in print to this point have been based on nothing more than wild speculation rooted for the most part in Ash Upson's misrepresentations of fiction as fact.

Billy the Kid should be remembered for whom he was. But then, who was he? Was he Henry McCarty, alias William H. Bonney? Every serious historian believes that to be the case. Could they be wrong? In all the interviews given by Billy the Kid's friends and acquaintances, not one ever mentioned the name McCarty. That is of course except Pat Garrett and his ghost writer Ash Upson. They brought the McCarty name to the attention of the whole world in their book. Why would we believe this duo?

Why do not any of the court records mention that Billy's name was Henry McCarty? In the final court document issued before his death, his death decree, he is identified six times by the phrase "William Bonny, alias Kid, alias William Antrim". Why not by his "real" name? Pat Garrett supposedly knew it – at least he revealed it in his book. Did he just forget to tell the court?

When Billy wrote the letter to Governor Lew Wallace revealing his Antrim aliases and declaring that his stepfather's name was Antrim, why didn't he come clean as to his real name – instead of just signing it William H. Bonney? What was the purpose of hiding his McCarty identity? He was in far more trouble as William H. Bonney than as Henry McCarty. Could he have been protecting his McCarty family? That's very unlikely since the only blood relative he would have had still living was his brother Joseph McCarty, who by the way wasn't even using the McCarty name. He had adopted his stepfather's Antrim surname.

There is a fascinating "story" that recounts a chance meeting between Joseph and Pat Garrett at the Armijo House in Trinidad Colorado in August of 1882. Joseph had heard that Pat had shot his brother and had "vowed to shoot Pat Garrett on sight". As the story goes, "Joseph and Garrett sat alone in the establishment and talked for almost two hours; they rose from their chairs, shook hands and departed. Later, someone asked Joseph what happened. Joseph remarked that he now had a better understanding of what happened." What was it that Joseph better understood? Was it that it was not his brother Henry McCarty that Pat had shot and killed?

On the 1880 Georgetown census, we find a 21 year old William McCarty who just happens to be living next door to Ed Moulton, an old friend of Mrs. Catherine McCarty and William H. Antrim back in their Silver City days. When Henry McCarty broke out of jail in Silver City in 1875, after being arrested for stealing clothes from a Chinese laundry, he spent time with Ed Moulton in Georgetown before going to Arizona.

Some distance away, but still in Georgetown is Chauncey Truesdell, a boyhood friend of Henry McCarty. Chauncey is in the household of his mother who had re-married to George W. Holt.

Five doors away from Chauncey and his mother is the household of Daniel Charles Casey. His wife is Mary P. Richards, Henry McCarty's former school teacher in Silver City.

Five doors away from Ed Moulton and six doors away from William McCarty, we also find Charles Nicoli with whom Chauncey Truesdell and Joseph Antrim (McCarty), Henry's brother, are said to have stayed with for a time.

What a cast of characters we find in 1880 Georgetown. Coincidence? You be the judge. Could this 21 year old William McCarty be Henry McCarty as in William Henry McCarty, alias Billy the Kid?

There is very little history recorded on Billy the Kid between June, 1879 and October, 1880 and most of that is hearsay and speculation. The few times that his name is mentioned seems to be pure hearsay and it is very doubtful that it was Henry McCarty. So, it is extremely likely that the William McCarty recorded on the 1880 census in Georgetown, is the same person that history has repeatedly recorded as Billy the Kid, right or wrong.

Then again, maybe this William McCarty was not Billy the Kid. In this same 1880 census, we find William Bonny (Bonney) living in the same dwelling as Charlie and Manuela Bowdre, while William McCarty was living in Georgetown. The census was taken in Fort Sumner and Georgetown at the exact same time, June 7, 8, and 9, 1880, so this William McCarty and William Bonny were two different people.

So, wasn't a William Bonney supposed to be Billy the Kid and wasn't he living with Charlie Bowdre and his wife. There can be little doubt that he could have very well been the William H. Bonney that history recorded as being shot to death by Pat Garrett in Pete Maxwell's bedroom in 1881. But did history get it right? You decide.

At this point, you are probably thinking; how many William McCartys lived in Georgetown that were friends with Ed Moulton and all being the same age. You just have to believe beyond a reasonable doubt that these William McCartys were one and the same person.

And, then, along comes a letter written by a Mr. Edward E Furman to the Governor of New Mexico, L. A. Sheldon. The letter basically listed citizens of Georgetown, Grant County, New Mexico who volunteered to fight Indians and preserve order in the county. Included on this list of citizens of Georgetown was a William McCarty. That in itself is not too unusual knowing that a William McCarty had been a citizen of Georgetown. The unusual thing about the letter was that it was written on September 10, 1881; almost two months after Billy the Kid was killed by Pat Garrett.

Might it be that William H. Bonney, alias Kid, alias William Antrim was really William H. Bonney? Wouldn't that be something if Billy the Kid turned out to be the William H. Bonney he claimed to be, the William H. Bonney his friends believed him to be, and the William H. Bonney the courts believed him to be?

I am merely suggesting here that it might be a bit premature to consider as settled, the question of Billy the Kid's identity. Henry McCarty is without a doubt a strong possibility. I would even agree that it is even probable. However, there remain many unanswered questions and no clear documented link between Henry McCarty and William H. Bonney, alias Billy the Kid. There were certainly newspaper accounts of the demise of the "Kid" that made such a link. But can we believe what we read in the newspaper? The most comprehensive such account I have found is one written two weeks after the fact by Singleton Mercer Ashenfelter in a Silver City newspaper published by him. It begins as follows:

**S. M. ASHENFELTER,**
**Editor and Proprietor.**

**Saturday, July 28, 1881**

**EXIT "THE KID"**

**The Fugitive Murderer Hunted Down and Killed by Sheriff Garrett.**

**The vulgar murderer and desperado known as "Billy the Kid" has met his just desires at last. He was shot and killed at the house of Pete Maxwell, near Fort Sumner, at midnight Thursday, the 14th instant, by Sheriff Pat Garrett of Lincoln County. He was a native of New York City, of Irish Parenting and his real name was William McCarthy, although he had been known as Henry Antrim, Billy Bonney, and other aliases. He lived in this city for some years with his mother Mrs. Antrim, who has since died, and began his criminal life by acts of petty**

**larceny. He escaped from jail and grew from bad to worse...**

What more proof could we want? S. M. Ashenfelter solved the mystery two weeks after the Kid's death! But where did Ashenfelter get his information? Might it have been a press release issued by Ash Upson? Or might Upson have depended on Ashenfelter for his background information on the Kid. Which came first, the chicken or the egg? Upson certainly had no credibility. Did S. M. Ashenfelter have any? Well, let's see. He thought the Kid's last name was McCarthy, not McCarty. He would surely have mentioned "Mrs. Antrim's" first name if he had known it. He writes that the Kid "lived in this city for some years with his mother Mrs. Antrim, who has since died,…" The time period that elapsed between their arrival in Silver City in the summer of 1873 and Catherine's death on September 16th 1874 does not qualify them as having lived there "for some years" as Ashenfelter characterized it. Could it be just sloppy reporting? Maybe, but where does the slop begin and end? Ashenfelter goes on to write in this article that:

**Since his escape from the Lincoln jail he had allowed his beard to grow, and had stained his skin to look like a Mexican.**

I don't believe any serious historian believes this. Ashenfelter closes with the statement that:

**Although only in his twenty-fourth year he had been guilty of many murders.**

That would make the Kid a little older than most scholars are willing to concede. That would have made him a 17 year old fourth grader in 1874. Lastly, we must keep in mind that S. M. Ashenfelter's day job was that of an attorney. He had earlier tried a series of cases at Fort Union involving "carrying whiskey into Indian Country." The result was summarized as follows, "The cases were all dismissed because of the ineptitude of U.S. District Attorney S. M. Ashenfelter." So who and what can we believe?

Was Henry McCarty the son of Mrs. Catherine McCarty Antrim, or some other kin, or no kin at all, and was he really the William H, Bonney, alias Billy the Kid, that we have always read about? I believe the answer is out there just waiting to be uncovered, or maybe just pieced together, and I think that we are getting close to finding it. There are just too many great historians out there that are interested in getting to the truth and I think very soon that one of them will say beyond any doubt, his "Real Name Was...."

*To be continued........*

# LIST OF APPENDICES

# APPENDIX A

## John Miller's Death Certificate

# APPENDIX B

## Isadora Miller's Death Certificate

# APPENDIX C

## Marriage Certificate for Catherine McCarty and William Antrim

# APPENDIX D

## William Henry Roberts alias Oliver L 'Brushy Bill' Roberts' Family Tree

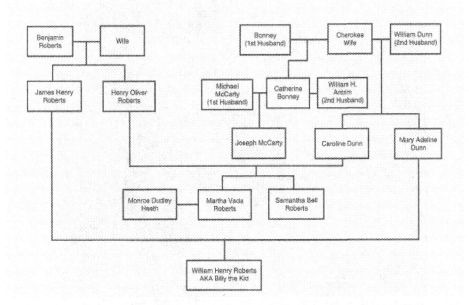

# APPENDIX E

## Oliver Pleasant Roberts/Anna Lee
## Marriage Certificate

# APPENDIX F

## Divorce Suit - Oliver Pleasant Roberts Vs. Anna Lee Roberts

# APPENDIX G

## Witness Summons - Oliver Pleasant Vs. Anna Lee Roberts

# APPENDIX H

## Summons for Anna Lee Roberts
## to Appear for Law Suit

THE STATE OF TEXAS

To the Sheriff or any Constable of Van Zandt    County, GREETING:

YOU ARE HEREBY COMMANDED TO SUMMON
Annie Roberts

to be and appear before the Honorable District Court of Van Zandt
County, Texas, at the next regular term thereof, to be held at the
Court House in Canton, Texas, on the 6th Monday after the 1st Monday in September    A. D. 1910    same being the    17    day
of    October    A. D. 1910    then and there to answer a Petition,
filed in said Court on the    17    day of September    A. D. 1910
wherein

G.P.Roberts is
                                                        Plaintiff    and

Annie Roberts is

Defendant    File number of said suit being No.3155
The nature of Plaintiff's Demand is as follows, to-wit:
Suit for divorce on the grounds of cruel treatment.
            Plaintiff and Defendant were lawfully married to each other in
Van Zandt County, Texas on the 11th day of July A.D.1909 and continued
to live together as man and wife until on or about the 1st of September A.D.1910, when Defendant left the home of this Plaintiff,and since
said time they have lived seperate and apart.That while they so lived
together as husband and wife,Plaintiff was good and kind to Defendant,
and did all in his power to make their said marriage a happy and
contented one,but the Defendant was unmindful of this kind treatment
and did all in her power to render Plaintiff unhappy;that she would
not cook for Plaintiff,and would stay gone and was permitted Plaintiff
to go to his work without having anything to eat;that she would visit
over the community among relatives and neighbors and would not tell
plaintiff whereshe was going,and when plaintiff would inquire of her
where she was going she would tell him that it was none of his
business;that Defendant would say hard things about Plaintiff's
mother;that she would talk about plaintiff to her neighbors and tell
plaintiff that she did not get the one that she loved,and would do all
in her power to make plaintiff jealous.Defendant would buy things that
she did not need and have them charged to plaintiff,saying that she
was going to keep plaintiff poor;that she bought a number of articles
and had them charged to plaintiff that she never brought home.
            Plaintiff prays that Defendant be cited to answer this
petition,and that at a final hearing hereof he have judgment dissolv-

# APPENDIX I

## Decree of Divorce for Oliver Pleasant and Anna Lee Roberts

# APPENDIX J

## Marriage Record - Oliver Pleasant Roberts and Mollie Brown

# APPENDIX K

## Marriage License - Oliver P. Roberts and Mollie Brown

# APPENDIX L

## Oliver Pleasant Roberts Draft Registration Card

# APPENDIX M

## Death Certificate - Luticia Roberts

# APPENDIX N

## Marriage Record for O. L. Roberts and Malinda E. Allison

# APPENDIX O

## Ollie L. Roberts Death Certificate

# APPENDIX P

## New Mexico Area Map - Billy the Kid Country

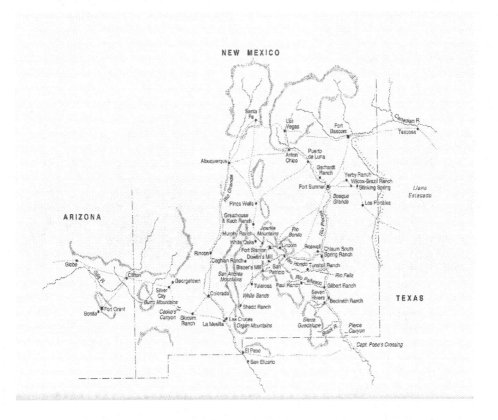

# APPENDIX Q

## Lincoln County, NM Courthouse, 1884

# APPENDIX R

## Maxwell House - Fort Sumner, NM

# APPENDIX S

## Fort Sumner Area Map - Billy the Kid Country

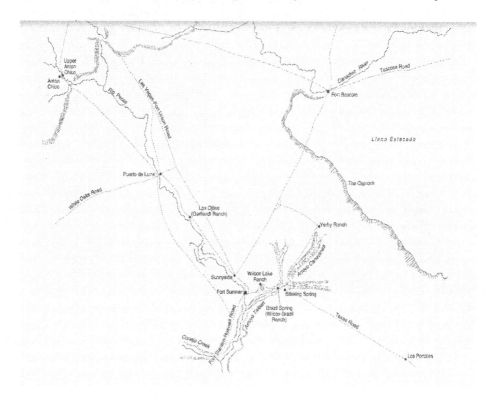

# APPENDIX T

*December 16, 1987*

*Dear Sir: the reason you are not finding my family is you don't have the right name. My grandfather was H.O. Roberts married to Shara (I think she meant Sarah)Elizabeth Ferguson on May 14, 1876. Oliver P. Roberts was Brushy Bill's name. I don't know what the P. was for. He was born August 26, 1879. I have the family Bible record. My husband thinks I should not tell you anything unless I know just what are your interests in my family? A William A. Tunstill P.O. Box 995 Roswell New Mex 88201 is also writing me asking questions which I have not written. He also has come up with a Ben Roberts as my great grandfather who was from (Kentucky?)and settled near Austin, 1835. I would also like for this to be settled as I know my uncle Oliver was not Billy the Kid.*

*Mrs. Geneva Pittmon*

This is a typed version of the handwritten letter from Brushy Bill's niece, Mrs. Geneva Pittmon to the Billy the Kid Gang founder Joe Bowlin.

# APPENDIX U

## Register for Joseph Roberts
### First Generation

1. **Joseph Roberts** was born in Virginia. He died in 1858 in Rusk Co., TX.

Joseph married **Rachel Henson** daughter of James Baret Henson and Elizabeth Ann Talley on 28 Jul 1844 in Rusk Co., TX. Rachel was born on 11 Sep 1828 in Rabun or Gilmer Co., GA.

They had the following children:

| | | | |
|---|---|---|---|
| + | 2 M | i. | **Virgil A. Roberts** was born in Mar 1847. |
| + | 3 F | ii. | **Amanda Roberts** was born on 29 Jul 1849. She died on 12 Jan 1923. |
| + | 4 F | iii. | **Samantha E. Roberts** was born in Jun 1850. |
| + | 5 M | iv. | **Henry Oliver Roberts** was born in May 1852. He died in 1924. |
| + | 6 M | v. | **Andrew B. Roberts** was born on 17 Oct 1854. He died on 24 Aug 1910. |

### Second Generation

5. **Henry Oliver Roberts** (Joseph) was born in May 1852 in Rusk Co., TX. He died in 1924 in
Van Zandt Co., TX. He was buried in 1924 in Hillcrest Cemetery, Van Zandt Co., TX.

Henry married (1) **Caroline Dunn** daughter of Francis Dunn and Eva Talitha Counts about 1871 in Arkansas. Caroline was born in Oct 1850 in Prairie, Franklin Co., AR. She died about 1874 in Arkansas.

Oliver married (2) They had the following children:

| | | | |
|---|---|---|---|
| + | 31 F | i. | **Samantha Belle Roberts** was born in Oct 1872. |
| + | 32 F | ii. | **Martha Vada Roberts** was born on 3 Sep 1873. She died on 10 Dec 1947. |

Henry married (2) **Sara Elizabeth Ferguson** daughter of John W. Ferguson and Martha Bolinger on 14 May 1876 in Arkansas. Sara was born on 24 Feb 1856. She died in 1924 in Van Zandt Co., TX. She was buried in 1924 in Hillcrest Cemetery, Van Zandt Co., TX.

They had the following children:

| | | | |
|---|---|---|---|
| + | 33 M | iii. | **Andrew Berry Roberts** was born on 9 Feb 1877. |
| | 34 F | iv. | **Mary C. Roberts** was born about 1878 in Bates, Sebastian Co., AR. |
| | 35 M | v. | **Oliver Pleasant Roberts** was born on 26 Aug 1878 in Bates, Sebastian Co., AR. He died on 27 Dec 1950 in Hico, Hamilton Co., TX. |

Oliver married (1) **Anna Lee** on 11 Jul 1909 in Van Zandt Co., TX and they divorced 10 Nov 1910. Anna was born about 1888 in Texas.

Oliver married (2) **Mollie Brown** on 21 Aug 1912 in Van Zandt Co., TX. Mollie was born about 1873 in Coleman, Texas. She died about 1919 in Van Zandt Co., TX.

Oliver married (3) **Luticia Ballard** daughter of Jesse W. Ballard and Samantha about 1929 in Van Zandt Co., TX. Luticia was born on 13 Jul 1875 in Stoddard Co., MO. She died on 22 Jun 1944 in Van Zandt Co., TX.

Oliver married (4) **Melinda E. Allison** on 14 Jan 1945 in Hamilton Co., TX. Melinda died in 1952 in Temple, Texas.

36 M  vi. **John W. Roberts** was born on 17 Jun 1881 in Bates, Sebastian Co., AR. He died on 11 Sep 1882 in Bates, Sebastian Co., AR. He was buried in Mount Harmony Cemetery, Greenwood, Sebastian Co., AR.

37 M  vii. **Lonnie V. Roberts** was born on 6 Jun 1884 in Sebastian Co., AR. He died on 30 Sep 1887 in Hopkins Co., TX. He was buried in Miller Grove Cemetery, Hopkins Co., TX.

\+ 38 M  viii. **Thomas Ulyce Roberts** was born on 3 Oct 1885. He died in 1958.

39 F  ix. **Nora Roberts** was born on 29 Apr 1892 in Hopkins Co., TX. She died on 6 May 1893 in Hopkins Co., TX. She was buried in Miller Grove Cemetery, Hopkins Co., TX.

\+ 40 M  x. **Joseph Irvin Roberts** was born on 26 Feb 1895.

# BIBLIOGRAPHY SOURCES

## Books/Newspapers

Adams, Ramon F. *A Fitting Death for Billy the Kid* University of Oklahoma Press, 1960

Airy, Helen *Whatever Happened to Billy the Kid?* Sunstone Press, 1993

Ballert, Marion with Breihan, Carl W. *Billy the Kid, A Date With Destiny* Superior Publishing Company, 1970

Burns, Walter Noble *The Saga of Billy the Kid* Longmeadow Press, 1992

Cline, Donald *Alias Billy the Kid, The Man Behind the Legend* Sunstone Press, 1986

*Dallas Morning News*

Edwards, Harold L. *Goodbye Billy the Kid* Creative Publishing Company, 1995

Garrett, Pat F. *The Authentic Life of Billy the Kid* University of Oklahoma Press, 1954

Jameson, W. C. *Billy the Kid, Beyond the Grave* Taylor Trade Publishing, 2005

Jameson, W. C. and Bean, Frederic *The Return of the Outlaw, Billy the Kid* Republic of Texas Press, 1998

Koop, W. E. *Billy the Kid, The Trail of a Kansas Legend*, 1965

Nolan, Frederick *The West of Billy the Kid* University of Oklahoma Press, 1998

Pena, Abe M. *Memories of Cibolo*

Russell, Randy *Billy the Kid, The Story - The Trial* The Crystal Press, 1994

Siringo, Charles A. *History of Billy the Kid* University of New Mexico Press, 2000

Sonnichsen, C. L. and Morrison, William V. *Alias Billy the Kid* University of New Mexico Press, 1955

*The Handbook of Texas*

Tunstill, William A. *Billy the Kid and Me Were the Same* 1988

Unknown *A Memorial and Biographical History of Hill County* 1892

Valdez, Dr. Jannay P. and Hefner, Judge Bobby E. *Billy the Kid: Killed in New Mexico --Died in Texas* Back Porch Publishers, Ink, 1994

*Wichita Tribune*

*Wichita Weekly Eagle*

## Libraries/Archives/County and State Records/Historical Societies/Museums **

Billy the Kid Museum, Canton, TX

Billy the Kid Museum, Fort Sumner, NM

Billy the Kid Museum, Hico, TX

Billy the Kid Museum, Old Fort Sumner, NM

Center for Regional Studies, University of New Mexico, Albuquerque, NM

Center for Southwest Research, University of New Mexico, Santa Fe, NM

Eastern New Mexico University Archives, Roswell, NM

Fray Angelico Chavez History Library, Palace of the Governors, Santa Fe, NM

Hamilton County Clerk's Office, Hamilton, TX

Hubbard Museum of the American West, Lincoln, NM

New Mexico State Records Center and Archives, Santa Fe, NM

Old Lincoln County Courthouse Museum, Lincoln, NM

Rio Grande Historical Collections, New Mexico State University, Las Cruces, NM

Silver City Museum Archives, Silver City NM

Van Zandt County Clerk's Office, Canton, TX

Van Zandt County Historical Society, Canton, TX
Western New Mexico University Archives, Silver City, NM

## Internet Sources

ancestry.com
rootsweb.com

**The locations in New Mexico were visited, but for this book, little or no information was used.

# INDEX

## E

Ealy, Mary, 32
East, James, 46
Edwards, Harold L., 98, 129
El Paso, TX, 63, 68, 69, 89
Ellis, Issac, 32
England, 23
Evans, Jesse, 18, 20, 21, 22, 38, 39

## F

Feliz River, NM, 21, 23
Fisher, Miles, 21
Fort Grant, AZ, 19, 20
Fort Sill, 7, 9, 10
Fort Smith, AR, 64, 68, 80
Fort Stanton, NM, 23, 40, 49, 54
Fort Sumner, NM, vii, 3, 4, 5, 11,
    37, 38, 41, 42, 43, 44, 45, 46,
    53, 54, 55, 56, 59, 60, 62, 64,
    87, 100, 101, 105, 129
Fort Worth, Texas, 67
Fountain, Colonel Albert J., 40,
    41, 48, 88
French, 'Big Jim', 27, 29, 32, 33,
    34, 89

## G

Gallop Independent, 3
Gallup, NM, 2
Garcia, 54
Garcia, Hijinio, 54
Garrett, Apolonaria Gutierrez, 56,
    59
Garrett, Pat, v, 2, 3, 4, 5, 11, 42,
    43, 44, 45, 46, 47, 48, 49, 50,
    53, 54, 55, 56, 59, 60, 61, 62,
    87, 88, 91, 93, 98, 99, 100,
    101, 129
Gates, Susan, 32, 34

Gauss, Godfrey, 21, 51, 52
Georgetown, NM, 2, 3, 11, 19, 92,
    100
Gerhardt, John, 46
Germany, 3, 4
Geronimo, 7, 9
Gila Ranch, AZ, 18, 63, 85
Gilbert, Bob, 27
Gladewater, TX, 72
Globe, AZ, 19, 63
Gonzales, Ignacio, 32, 35
Grand Saline, Texas, 63
Grant County, NM, 2, 22, 92
Greathouse, Jim, 41, 42
Greathouse-Kuch Station, 42
Greer County, TX (OK), 10, 11
Grzelachowski, Alexander, 46
Guadalupe Mountains, NM, 20
Gutierrez, Celsa, 56, 59, 60, 62, 88
Gutierrez, Jose Delores, 56
Gutierrez, Saval, 56, 59, 60

## H

Hall, Lee, 7, 43, 95
Hamilton County, TX, 15, 82, 88,
    129
Harmon County, OK, 10
Hefner, Bobby, 72, 81, 84, 85, 129
Hico, Hamilton County, TX, vi,
    vii, 73, 82, 83, 129
Hill, John, 4, 8
Hill, Tom, 26
Hindman, George, 28, 29, 38
Holbrook, AZ, 5
Holt, George W., 100
Hopkins County, TX, 80
Hotel de Luna, 19, 20
Houston, Sam, 13, 77, 83
Hudgens, Will, 43
Humboldt, KS, 92
Hunter Mortuary, 9

# I

Idaho Trail, 64
Indian Jim, 63, 64, 66, 67, 68, 71, 83
Indian Territory (Oklahoma), 10, 13, 16, 17, 19, 63, 64, 65, 68, 69, 72, 83, 84, 93
Indianapolis, IN, 14, 15, 83

# J

Jackson, Georgie Conley, 6
James, Frank, 13
James, Jesse, 13
Jameson, W. C., 79, 84
Jaralozo, Valencia County, NM, 8
Jennings, Al, 65, 66
Jones Ranch, 21
Jones, Jim, 21
Jones, John, 21, 34, 35, 49

# K

Kansas City, KS, 64, 65
Ketchum, 21
Kimbrel, Sheriff, 40, 41, 42
Kinney, John, 22, 32, 34
Kiowa Indians, 7, 10
Knight family, 18
Knight, Mrs., 20
Koop, W. E., 96, 129
Kuch, Fred, 43

# L

La Junta, NM, 25
Lambson, Appollas, 4
Lambson, Eugene, 4
Lambson, Hesseltine, 4
Las Tablas, NM, 54
Las Vegas, NM, 2, 8, 39, 41, 46, 48

Lee, Anna, 125
Leonard, Ira, 40, 41, 42, 47
Lexington, KY, 13
Liberty, AZ, 6, 8
Lincoln County War, vi, 3, 25, 35, 37
Llano County, Texas, 30
Lloyd, Dick, 27
Lobato, Frank, 62, 88
Long, Jack, 29
Longworth, Tom, 43
Los Lunas, NM, 4
Loving's Bend, NM, 20, 85

# M

Mackie, John R., 19
Maricopa, AZ, 7
Martinez, Atanacio, 38
Mason County, Texas, 30
Mason, Barney, 53, 54, 55, 88
Mathews, Billy, 28, 29, 39
Maxwell, Deluvina, 46
Maxwell, Dona Luz, 46
Maxwell, Lucien B., 2
Maxwell, Pete, 2, 4, 5, 87, 100, 101
Maxwell, Ramon, 2
McCarty, Henry, vi, vii, 11, 13, 14, 15, 16, 17, 18, 19, 20, 21, 22, 63, 84, 85, 86, 90, 92, 94, 95, 98, 99, 100, 101, 102
McCarty, Michael, 84, 91
McCarty, William, 3, 11, 100
McCloskey, William, 27, 28
McClure, Tony, 65, 76
McCullum, Frank, 39
McDaniel, Jimmy, 20
McGaffey, NM, 3
McKinney, Kip, 43
McKinney, TX, 17
McNab, Frank, 21, 26, 27, 28, 29

McSween, Alexander. 23, 31, 32, 33, 34, 35, 37, 39, 41, 53
McSween, Susan, 31, 33, 38, 39
Meadows, John, 54
Mescalero-Apache Reservation Agency, 37, 38
Mesilla Valley, NM, 20
Mesilla, NM, 18
Middleton, John, 21, 25, 27, 28, 29, 30
Miller, Isadora, 2, 4, 5, 6, 8, 9, 11, 105
Miller, John, v, vi, vii, 1, 2, 3, 4, 5, 6, 7, 8, 9, 10, 11, 99, 100, 105
Miller, Max, 2, 6, 8, 66
Mobile, AL, 69
Moore, Scott, 48
Mormons, 5
Morris, Harvey, 31, 33, 34
Morris, J., 17
Morton, Billy, 20, 21, 25, 26, 27, 28, 89
Moulton, Ed, 19, 63, 100
Mountain Bill, 18, 68, 85
Murdock, Colonel Marsh, 96
Murphey, John, 20
Murphy, Lawrence, 21, 22, 23, 25, 28, 30, 31, 33, 37, 41
Muskogee, OK, 69

## N

Nacogdoches, TX, 13
Nash, Joe, 35
Nation's Ranch, NM, 65, 76
Navajo Indians, 2
Neis, Tony, 47
New Orleans, LA, 97, 98
New York City, NY, 93, 94, 95, 97, 98, 101
Newcomb, John, 26
Nicoli, Charles, 100

Nolan, Frederick, vii, 85, 97, 99, 129
Norris, Tom, 54
North Canadian River, IT, 68
North Fork of the Red River, 10
North Platte, Nebraska, 64, 67

## O

O'Folliard, Tom, 32, 34, 37, 38, 40, 41, 43, 44, 45
O'Keefe, Tom, 20, 22, 85
Oklahoma City, OK, 66, 67
Olinger, Bob, 47, 48, 49, 50, 51, 52, 53
Ozark Jack, 65
Ozark Mountains, 65
Ozark Trail, MO, 64

## P

Padilla, Juan, 54
Page, NM, 3
Pajarito Springs, NM, 25
Paris, TX, 17
Parker, Judge, 64, 65, 67, 68, 80
Patron, Juan, 32, 34, 39, 41
Pawnee Bill, 68
Pecos River, 22, 27, 49
Peña, Abe M., 2
Pendleton, Oregon, 67, 76
Peppin, George, 29, 31, 32
Perry, Sam, 77
Phoenix, AZ, 6
Phoenix, NM, 20, 85
Pickett, Tom, 43, 44
Pinkerton detectives, 64, 68
Pioneer Home, vi, vii, 6, 7, 10
Pioneer Home Cemetery, 6
Poe, John William, 5
Portales, NM, 7, 38
Powell River Valley, TN, 79